SOPHOCLES

Antigone

translated by
DON TAYLOR

with commentary and notes by
ANGIE VARAKIS

B L O O M S B U R Y
NEW DELHI • LONDON • OXFORD • NEW YORK • SYDNEY

BLOOMSBURY INDIA
Bloomsbury Publishing India Pvt. Ltd
Second Floor, LSC Building No. 4, DDA Complex, Pocket C – 6 & 7,
Vasant Kunj, New Delhi, 110070

BLOOMSBURY, METHUEN DRAMA INDIA and the Diana logo
are trademarks of Bloomsbury Publishing Plc

First published in India 2017
This edition first published in the United Kingdom in 2006
by Methuen Publishing Ltd
Reissued with a new cover in 2010
Reprinted by Bloomsbury Methuen Drama 2010, 2011, 2013, 2014, 2015,
2016 (Three times), 2017

This translation of Antigone first published 1986 by Eyre Methuen Ltd in Sophocles:
The Theban Plays (subsequently Sophocles plays: one)

ISBN: PB: 978-93-86349-10-1
6 8 10 9 7

For sale in the Indian subcontinent only

Series: Student Editions
Typeset by SX Composing DTP, Rayleigh, Essex
Printed and bound in India by Gopsons Papers Pvt. Ltd., Noida

MIX
Paper | Supporting responsible forestry
FSC® C191020

To find out more about our authors and books visit www.bloomsbury.com and sign up for our newsletters

Contents

Sophocles: *c.* 496–406 BC

Sophocles' long life and prolific career as a dramatist (over 120 plays) coincides with the unfolding of fifth-century Athenian democracy, that high classical period, which witnessed wars with both Persia and Sparta, Pericles' golden years of democratic rule, the building and decoration of the Parthenon, an unprecedented acceleration in philosophy, science and the arts. Sophocles outlived the younger playwright Euripides and met such figures as the dramatist Aeschylus, the politician Pericles, the philosopher Socrates, the historians Herodotus and Thucydides and many others. On a personal level, he is said to have married one Nicostrate and fathered a son Iophon with whom he allegedly had a bad relationship. He also had a grandson who was named after him.

Our biographical information about Sophocles is related more to his life outside the theatre since most of his plays are lost, while the dates of his surviving seven dramas are uncertain (out of the seven plays that survive entire we only have fixed dates for *Philoctetes* (409) and *Oedipus at Colonus* (401)). However, most scholars agree that there are good stylistic reasons for placing *Ajax* and *Women of Trachis* in the early period of his career (late 440s and late 430s respectively) and *Electra* at a much later date (possibly about 415). *Oedipus the King* is most commonly placed in the early 420s while *Antigone* is more confidently positioned between 442 and 440 due to the claim that Sophocles was elected general around 440 after his success with his production of *Antigone*.

All of the tragedies mentioned in the chronology were produced at the City Dionysia festival, an annual event to honour the gods and display Athens' wealth and prosperity. Information regarding Sophocles' personal life relies mainly on various anecdotal sources which were compiled in later antiquity into a biography entitled *The Life of Sophocles*. This chronology has confined itself to those dates which are most trustworthy.

496/5 Sophocles, son of Sophillos, is born into a wealthy family of merchants at the *deme* (locality) of Colonus, near Athens. As a young boy he must have received the usual aristocratic education which involved training in music, dancing and athletics.

490 The first Persian invasion at Marathon is defeated by the Athenian navy. It is said that the tragedian Aeschylus participated in this battle.

480 The second Persian invasion is defeated by the Athenian navy at Salamis. Sophocles, already known for his talent in the performing arts, is invited to participate in the victory song celebrating the Athenian military success. The youngest out of the three famous tragic poets, Euripides, is born.

468 Sophocles enters the drama competition at the City Dionysia festival (possibly with the play *Triptolemos*) and is awarded first prize, defeating the elder and already established tragedian Aeschylus. Sophocles' successful debut makes him instantly popular.

462 The political leaders Pericles and Ephialtes reform the Athenian constitution giving more power to the people against the aristocratic few. The golden age of democracy is about to begin. Sophocles may not have been in favour of such radical reforms against traditional values.

458 Aeschylus' trilogy *Oresteia* is presented, reflecting in a positive way the current political situation.

449 The competition for actors in tragedy is introduced at the City Dionysia.

late 440s Sophocles' play *Ajax* is presented.

c. 445 The comic playwright Aristophanes is born.

443/2 Sophocles serves as *Hellenotamias* (treasurer of the Athenian empire). His position in public office reveals that he was not only a successful tragedian but also a politically active citizen.

442–40 Sophocles wins first prize with his production of *Antigone*. Such is the popularity of the play that Sophocles is elected general during an expedition against the island of Samos (Samian War, 440 BC), serving alongside Pericles.

438 Sophocles for the first time defeats the younger poet Euripides and is awarded first prize.

431–04 A less optimistic period begins, that of the Peloponnesian War and the gradual decline of the Athenian empire. During the second summer of the war, in a city overcrowded with refugees from the Spartan invasion, plague raged and persisted over the next few years. Pericles is believed to have been one of the victims (in 429). The events of the war must have inspired and influenced many of Sophocles' later plays.

late 430s During this period of change and uncertainty Sophocles' *Women of Trachis* is presented, perhaps the most Euripidean of his surviving plays.

mid 420s *Oedipus the King* is awarded second prize. Sophocles poses questions in the play regarding fate and personal choice, revealing a rather critical attitude towards the Athenian 'enlightment' (Pericles' golden years).

420/19 Sophocles becomes priest of the cult of the god Asclepios, or cult of the Healing Hero, showing that he was indeed a religious man. He is thought to have provided an altar for the god at his own home when the cult was first introduced to Athens until a proper public shrine could be built. Less certain is the belief that Sophocles himself was worshipped as a hero under the name Dexion (receiver of the god) after his death.

?415 In the later stages of his career his play *Electra* is presented, which again demonstrates the strong commitment of an unmarried heroine to her father (Agamemnon) and brother (Orestes).

415–13 Sicilian Expedition. The Athenians suffer total defeat in Sicily (413) and Sophocles is called to serve as *proboulos* (special state commissioner) in the emergency situation.

409 Sophocles wins first prize with his play *Philoctetes.*

406 Sophocles dies in Athens.

404 Peace between Athens and Sparta is signed. Rule of the Thirty Tyrants in Athens.

401 *Oedipus at Colonus* is produced posthumously by Sophocles' grandson, who is also a tragic poet. Due to its setting, Sophocles' birthplace, the play is believed to contain autobiographical elements.

Plot

Antigone, following the formal conventions of Greek tragedy, is composed of seven scenes (opening scene [*prologos*], five scenes and a final scene [*exodus*]), which are separated distinctly by six choral songs (opening lyric [*parodos*] and five choral songs [*stasima*]) which have some relevance to the dramatic situation.

The formality, cohesion and dramatic economy of the whole plot structure was not only second nature to the spectators and tragedians of ancient Greece but also a significant component upon which the play's success depended. As Aristotle observed in his monumental work of literary criticism, *Poetics,* much of the excitement of a tragic performance comes from the skilful structuring of the plot (*muthos*). In *Antigone*, the way in which the play is built through a series of climaxes and confrontations that culminate in the revelation of Creon's mistake and the disclosure of the multiple deaths is characteristic.

Opening scene (prologos)
The play opens with a dialogue scene between the two young sisters Antigone and Ismene. It is the morning after the Thebans have defeated the Argive army in an attack during which the brothers Eteocles and Polynices have killed one another. As a result their uncle Creon has assumed power and this is his first day of office.

The sisters are standing outside the royal palace at Thebes, the house that once belonged to their father Oedipus. Antigone is the first to speak, announcing to her sister the very first order Creon has given – that Polynices' body is to be denied burial though Eteocles, the defender of the city, has been buried with due honour. The proclamation will deny Polynices rest in the underworld and Antigone asks her sister to support her decision to defy the decree and give her brother the burial he deserves.

Ismene's answer reveals that she is cautious and lacking the courage of her sister. She reminds Antigone of their parents' ill fate, warning her that by defying the king and the power of the state they are in danger of suffering death by stoning. Antigone's failure to involve her sister in her plan does not affect her decision and she is now determined to carry out the act alone, willing to die for her convictions.

The scene ends with Ismene leaving through the central door of the stage building to wait in the palace and Antigone boldly heading off down one of the side-entrances to go and bury her brother.

First choral song (parodos)

The chorus enters from the other side-entrance. It consists of the elders of Thebes, who represent the community. The group of old men, unaware of Creon's proclamation, have come to celebrate the city's victory against the foreign invader. Their lyrics are full of images of light, echoing a visible joy. The men also describe in a dramatic manner the details of the previous day's fierce fight at the seven gates of Thebes and the way in which the two brothers met and killed one another at the last and seventh gate.

First scene (*First* epeisodion)

The new king is announced in a grand manner as responsible for the city's glorious achievement and he makes his entry. He speaks at length and with no interruption, dominating the whole stage with his presence. His inaugural address is a self-introduction containing words of political wisdom, revealing his devotion to the state and his determination to honour the citizens who serve the city and punish those who betray the country. He also announces the state decree he has issued concerning the sons of Oedipus, Polynices and Eteocles, and for the second time the horror of an exposed corpse is described, this time by the king; the sight which caused Antigone's revulsion is used by Creon as an exemplary punishment for traitors of the city.

The chorus supports Creon's stance, deferring to his authority which holds full power over the dead and the living. The new king orders the chorus to implement his edict and warns them against secretly plotting against him. Suddenly a soldier arrives unannounced, entering from where Antigone left. He is one of the guards who have been watching the corpse. At the beginning the frightened man hesitates to tell the whole truth and the only piece of information Creon can extract is that the corpse has miraculously vanished. Eventually and under increasing pressure from the king, the soldier reveals that the dead body has been 'lightly covered with a layer of earth'.

The chorus, unaware of Antigone's intention to bury her brother, suggests it is a warning from the gods, a natural reaction to an incredible story. Creon disregards the chorus's suggestion as foolish. With fury he claims that his initial fears of betrayal have come true and that the burial of the corpse is a political conspiracy. He accuses the soldier of complicity and threatens to punish him if he does not reveal the conspirators. The soldier departs to search for those responsible for breaking the law.

Second choral song (*First* stasimon)

The first *stasimon* is a song of praise to the miracle of man, describing his ability to work creatively upon his environment. Man's fate is seen within the context of the city. The lyric expands the meaning of the action to a broader level for the first time, but its praise of man's intellectual achievements and cultural advances will be qualified during the course of the play. The message of the song is not absolute; it could be interpreted as a warning, in particular against arrogance, which has relevance to Creon's behaviour later on.

Second scene (*Second* epeisodion)

Antigone is led on stage from the side-entrance under guard. The chorus cannot believe their eyes. The soldier proudly produces the perpetrator and in contrast to his first entrance is delighted to be there. He announces that he witnessed the girl performing the burial rites and gives a vivid description of the ceremony. Finally he claims that Antigone did not deny it.

Creon addresses Antigone directly for the first time posing a simple legal question, 'Are you guilty, or not?' Antigone proudly accepts responsibility for the burial and the soldier is discharged. She also admits that she was fully aware of Creon's proclamation but she consciously chose to follow the unwritten laws of the gods which stand above any human legal system. Antigone is proud of her action and is prepared to die for it.

Creon disagrees with Antigone's ideological position and stands on his dignity as a man, his authority as a king. He claims that even the most rigid spirits can break and ties of kinship are of no importance when measured against the power of the law. Finally he implicates Ismene, mistaking her signs of agitation outside for clear signs of complicity.

As we await the arrival of Ismene the dispute between Antigone and Creon intensifies, each argument tearing them further apart until the rift is fully defined and Antigone's death penalty confirmed. Ismene appears on stage under guard. She tries to stand proudly by her sister, announcing that she was her partner in the crime. Antigone however rejects her involvement claiming that simple words cannot count as actions and that she must concentrate on saving herself. Ismene desperately tries to persuade Creon to reconsider his decision to kill her sister bringing into her argument the intended marriage between Antigone and his son Haemon and pointing out their special love. Creon dismisses Ismene's appeal and the scene ends with Antigone and Ismene being dragged inside the palace by the guards and Creon remaining on stage for the duration of the choral song that follows.

Third choral song (*Second* stasimon)

The second *stasimon* is in evident contrast to the previous choral 'praise of man'. It reveals a new perception of man in relation to the gods. The chorus warns through an elaborate scheme of visual imagery that once a man has offended the gods his family will be doomed from generation to generation. The content of the song derives from Antigone's and her family's sealed fate. However Creon's presence on stage makes the spectator wonder whether his fate, which is yet to be determined, is also doomed.

Third scene (*Third* epeisodion)

The chorus announces Haemon's arrival from the palace, wondering whether he has come to plead for mercy for his bride. Creon greets his son with the certainty that Haemon is on his side. His speech towards Haemon highlights the importance of obedience, of citizens to their king, of women to men and sons to fathers. For this reason there is no question that Antigone who has disobeyed the authority of the state must be punished with death.

Haemon's response reveals that he is indeed concerned for the well-being of his father. However he has also come to let him know the opinion of the people of Thebes whose secret admiration for Antigone he discloses, trying to make his father realise his own political isolation. His final words are an appeal to Creon to reconsider, in effect, to see that the views of others may also have merit. Creon repeatedly accuses his son of being Antigone's slave and is determined she won't live to marry him. Haemon declares that when the state becomes one man it ceases to be a state. The bitter exchange of words between father and son is sealed with Haemon's announcement that his father will never see him again. The scene ends with Creon's detailed description of Antigone's punishment, walled up in a cave and buried alive, and his decision to free Ismene.

Fourth choral song (*Third* stasimon)
As Creon retires to arrange Antigone's punishment the chorus sings about the glory and victory of love and sexual attraction, a power that nobody mortal or immortal can escape. The content of the song follows naturally from the conclusion of the previous scene showing Haemon's devotion to the woman he loves.

Fourth scene (*Fourth* epeisodion)
The chorus announces Antigone's entrance, an isolated figure escorted by guards who are conducting her to the place where she is to meet death, her final walk from the sunlight to darkness as the bride of Hades, the god of the underworld. Her lament reveals her intense feeling of desolation, absolute loneliness, the loneliness of death. The chorus attempts to cheer her by reminding her of the glory she will achieve. The high emotion is suddenly interrupted by the re-entry of Creon who orders the guards to proceed with their work as quickly as possible. Antigone in a long speech addresses her grave and her dead brother, lamenting her fate, to Creon's frustration. At the conclusion of the scene Antigone is led away to her tomb.

Fifth choral song (*Fourth* stasimon)
The chorus sings of three other cases whose fate was similar to that

of Antigone. Antigone's fate becomes part of a historic pattern, infected by brutality and darkness.

Fifth scene (*Fifth* epeisodion)
The blind prophet Teiresias appears for the first time on stage led by a young boy, his guide. He has come to warn Creon that he is 'like a man balanced on a razor' and that he, Teiresias, has witnessed prophetic signs which show that the gods are angry at Creon's treatment of Polynices. Creon responds arrogantly and attacks the seer's integrity. Teiresias then prophesies disaster for the king and orders his guide to lead him away. The chorus accompanies his exit with words that reveal their deep worry about their king's future and finally persuades Creon to unearth Antigone.

Sixth choral song (*Fifth* stasimon)
The chorus sings a song to the patron god of Thebes, Dionysus. They ask the god for help, recollecting his rituals and ecstatic dancing which could cleanse Thebes from its pollution, bring peace and rest to a city full of anguish.

Final scene (exodus)
A messenger arrives who laments the fickleness of fortune and brings the horrible news of Antigone's and Haemon's deaths. Eurydice, Creon's wife, who overhears part of it, nearly faints but insists on hearing the whole truth. The messenger's next speech gives full details of the couple's deaths: Creon's discovery that Antigone has hanged herself and his confrontation with Haemon, Haemon unable to bear the death of his beloved cousin, committing suicide in front of his father's eyes.

Eurydice, having heard the messenger's long speech, walks into the palace in silence. Both the chorus and the messenger are worried by this and the messenger goes into the palace to see what has happened to her.

The final part of the scene and the climactic conclusion of the play starts with the announcement of Creon's return. Servants enter carrying the dead body of his son on a bier, with Creon following. As Creon, full of remorse, mourns for his son, the scene is interrupted by the arrival of the messenger from the palace bringing news of a further catastrophe and the palace doors open to reveal Eurydice, dead. Creon is in deep anguish but there is no escape for him, just a final comment by the chorus about how people eventually become wiser through suffering.

Commentary

The myth

In classical Greece the plot and characters of a tragedy were not invented from scratch each time the writer composed a new play. Sophocles had at his disposal a number of well-known legends and narratives closely aligned to the main values of his culture. Images and stories inspired by myths were connected with every form of artistic expression and ceremonial ritual, proving that the Greeks were not only familiar with a great number of mythical stories, but also made use of them to define themselves in the world and communicate their specific cultural issues. The myths were malleable and allowed for the writer to become inventive, composing versions that on many occasions had little to do with their oral or literary precedents. The myths could be described as the basic material, and characters were open to revision and invention with regard to characterisation, motivation, sequence of events or even location.

In tragic theatre, even though the stories were set in a distant Bronze Age, the characters were mentally close to the audience and shared the values of the democratic period in Athens. The mythic subject helped the writer retain critical distance, allowing his audience to judge current political or ideological issues in an objective manner. The geographical characteristics of the mythical location, which usually existed in reality, could also be used in the stories and affect the dramatic events of the play. For example, the real city of Thebes had seven gates and in *Antigone* fierce fighting takes place at the seven gates of the city. One should note, however, that a myth could not be completely overturned as it was also considered part of Greece's history. The two most significant myths that were used in most Greek tragedies and were also perceived as part of Greece's distant historical past were the Theban cycle with the events that surrounded the house of Laius, and the rival Trojan cycle with the events that concerned the house of King Agamemnon.

The story of Antigone is part of the legend of the house of Laius, king of Thebes, which also became a source of inspiration for two other surviving tragedies by Sophocles, *Oedipus the King* and *Oedipus at Colonus*. Even though the mythical sequence of events places Antigone's story at the end, the chronology in which the tragedies were written does not follow this order as the plays were not composed with the intention of being part of a trilogy: *Antigone* was written first, *Oedipus the King* second and *Oedipus at Colonus* last.

The Theban saga of Laius and his children was one of the most popular in the Greek literary and iconographic tradition and although one can never be entirely sure of a myth's original version, one can give a broad outline of the most important points which would have been familiar to Sophocles' audience when *Antigone* was first performed in 441 BC. The myth runs as follows: Laius, king of Thebes, and his wife Jocasta receive a prophecy from Apollo's oracle that their only son, Oedipus, will murder his father. Full of fear, they seek to defy the prophecy by leaving their infant to perish in an isolated place. However they do not realise that he survives. In accordance with the prophecy, the infant grows and unknowingly kills his father Laius, and marries his mother Jocasta by whom he has four children, two sons, Eteocles and Polynices, and two daughters, Ismene and Antigone. Discovering the horrible truth, Jocasta commits suicide and Oedipus blinds himself and eventually dies in exile. At some point during his life Oedipus curses his sons, pronouncing that they will kill each other. After Oedipus' death, Eteocles and Polynices agree that they will each rule Thebes as king in alternate years. During his time in exile, Polynices marries Argia, daughter of Adrastus, king of Argos. When after a year Eteocles refuses to abdicate, violating their original agreement, Polynices leads an army of Argives against Thebes to claim the throne for himself. A fierce battle ensues, after which the brothers meet and slay one another at the seventh gate of Thebes in accordance with their father's curse. With all male heirs of Laius dead, Creon, brother of Jocasta, takes over as king of Thebes and this is the point at which the story of Sophocles' *Antigone* begins.

In the next phase of the myth, which Sophocles did not deal with, Creon as ruler refuses to allow the Argives to recover their dead but is eventually compelled to change his mind through the intervention of Theseus and an Athenian army. At a later stage of the story the sons of the seven who died at the gates return to destroy Thebes.

A great number of important pre-Sophoclean literary versions dealt with the Theban saga, the most recent dramatic version to Sophocles' *Antigone* being Aechylus' trilogy *Laius*, *Oedipus* and the surviving tragedy *Seven Against Thebes*. Sophocles and his audience would have been fully conscious of these.

The festival

The tragedy of *Antigone* was presented in the Theatre of Dionysus as part of a drama competition that took place every year during the City (or Great) Dionysia, one of the city's numerous festivals.

The City Dionysia, which was dedicated to Dionysus, god of fertility, wine and theatre, was one of Athens' greatest annual festivals and aimed to celebrate the god's arrival in Athens as well as the city's wealth and prosperity. The event took place in mid to late March when seagoing again became possible after the winter. This meant that it was easy for foreign guests to visit the city and witness the festive activities. Another significant aspect of the timing of the event was the fact that the military campaigns and election of the ten generals took place soon after it ended; indeed the drama competitions could have had a strong influence upon current political decisions. For example, it is claimed that Sophocles himself was elected general because of his success with *Antigone*.

The radical democracy of Athens was reflected in the overall organisation of the festival which was an inclusive and participatory event. Although it is difficult to determine the precise order of the activities, a rough schedule of the festival can be made as it developed until the outbreak of the Peloponnesian War in 431 BC.

The day before the official beginning of the City Dionysia a pre-contest took place during which the poets and their casts (out of costume) described the plays they were due to perform in the drama competitions. The audience therefore were already informed about what they were expected to view in the following days.

The next morning the first day of the festival began and all normal life came to a halt. The wooden statue of Dionysus was led into the city escorted by young men carrying lighted torches, in a ceremony which represented the god's arrival in Athens. At the end of the evening procession the statue was positioned in a temple below the theatre of Dionysus where it remained for the duration of the festival.

The second day a great civic procession took place in which each citizen showed his civic status by a specific costume while the foreign guests were identified through scarlet robes. The sponsors of the drama performances (*choregoi*) were also marked out by wearing rich gowns. During this procession all citizens were included, typical not only of a democratic society but also of many Dionysiac cults. The procession included a number of dances (*dithyrambs*) performed by each tribe of Athens, and ended with the sacrifice of bulls at the altar below the theatre.

On the third day, the drama competitions commenced between three tragic poets and five comic poets. Before they began a piglet was sacrificed and its dead body carried around the performance area to purify the space in which the plays would be staged. The decision about who was to compete was made by a state official (*archon*) selected by lot about six months in advance. The same person allocated each poet to a wealthy sponsor chosen by the state. The sponsor's responsibility was to finance the whole production and the training of the chorus, as a form of taxation.

The drama competitions lasted four days. Dramatists presented three tragedies, a 'satyr' play, and a comedy each day. Sophocles is sometimes held to have been the first to abandon the form of the trilogy (three tragedies) to tell a single story (Aeschylus' *Oresteia* is the only surviving example). Instead he made each tragedy a complete entity in itself. However some people believe that Aeschylus in fact was the first with his tragedy *Persians* in 472, also the first surviving play to have been inspired by real events. Prizes were awarded to the poets and the actors (from 449 BC onwards) at the end of the festival by ten judges (a representative from each tribe), elected on the opening day of the festival by lot and sworn to impartiality.

The religious and civic activities that surrounded the productions must have created part of the play's meaning. In ancient Greece the viewing of a tragedy or comedy was not only a form of entertainment and education but also a religious as well as a public experience, which added to the play a political dimension and ritual quality.

It is obvious that the choral odes, laments and burial rites which are so often described in *Antigone* would have had an extra meaning for an audience surrounded by sacrificial rites and religious dances, while the significant political speeches of Creon would have reminded spectators of the famous orators who during the festival would have spoken of their glorious city's achievements with pride and dedication. Finally, the competitive nature of the event would have added a playful element as many spectators would have supported and cheered for their favourite poet or actor, participating in this way in the whole process. The art of persuasion (rhetoric) as expressed in fifth-century public speeches (in the assembly, the law courts, etc.) was also present in the theatre, not only for performers in their roles but also as actors and dancers trying to convince their audience that their performance and play deserved the first prize.

In 449 the competition for actors in tragedy was introduced at the City Dionysia and the actor gradually became as important as the dramatist. It might well have affected the way in which actors delivered their parts or even the way in which parts were composed by the tragic poet. For example, Aeschylus' early plays were more chorus-oriented and affirming of socio-political values while Sophocles places more emphasis on the individual (the Sophoclean hero) and the issue of personal choice (see pp. xxviii–xxix).

Political context

Antigone was first presented *c.* 440 BC, the interwar period (between the Persian and Spartan Wars), during which Athenian democracy was flourishing following the reforms of Pericles and Ephialtes (462), which ensured that political power belonged to the body of the citizens and not to the aristocratic few.

In 477 the Greek city states formed the Delian League for mutual protection from the Persians. Athens was placed at the head of it because of her power at sea. Initially its treasury was located on the island of Delos – hence the League's name – but Pericles transferred it to Athens, boosting the city's political and financial power and gradually transforming the federation into an Athenian empire. The increasing power and wealth of Athens were clearly reflected in the city's unprecedented achievements in science, philosophy and the arts as well as through its lavish expenditure on public festivals.

Within this climate of prosperity and optimism the body of Athenian citizens became increasingly aware of their power to create their own destiny and old values which had flourished in the sixth-century oligarchy, when the central institution had been the extended family – values such as the importance of blood-kinship – were challenged, something reflected in Creon's stance in *Antigone*. The foundation of Athenian democracy was based on Cleisthenes' reorganisation of the citizen body into ten local tribes or *demoi*, as opposed to family units, which meant the transition from a principle of kinship to that of locality (508/7). The new constitution even changed the way a man identified himself. For example, in his official designation his name was no longer followed by his patronymic but by the name of his tribe. Such radical incursions by political reformers into the sphere of private relationships show that the old loyalty to the family was considered a challenge to the new democratic institutions.

Some philosophers even challenged the power of the gods and their ability to affect human lives, claiming that humans had gradually become masters of their environment through the development of civilisation and the establishment of democracy. An example of this was the thinker Protagoras who declared that 'man was the measure of all things', an idea which is clearly reflected in *Antigone*'s first choral ode where man is praised for working creatively upon nature.

The best source from which one can get an idea of the Athenian political constitution and ideals of Athenian democracy is Pericles' famous funeral speech, as given by the historian Thucydides. The speech stresses the ideals of radical democracy, and praises the Athenian way of life, especially in contrast to the Spartan. It particularly highlights the importance of the people being involved in the city's affairs, accusing those who mind their own private business of being useless, and bringing to mind Creon's inaugural speech in *Antigone*.

However one can also argue that Pericles' speech rejects Creon's one-dimensional notion that man's nature is reduced to that of a useful member of a political unit with no human distinctiveness or personal emotions. Antigone's insistence throughout the play that the state acknowledges and approves the uniqueness of the individual is also expressed in Pericles' speech as one can see in the following extract:

> But while the law secures equal justice to all alike in their private disputes, the claim of excellence is also recognised; and when a citizen is

> in any way distinguished, he is preferred to the public service, not as a matter of privilege, but as a reward of merit. (Thucydides, II. 37.1, trans. Jowett, OUP, 1900)

Finally, not everybody was considered politically equal in democratic Athens. Slaves and women were excluded from all public and political institutions and had no right to vote. Slaves were used as labourers to build and preserve the wealth and strong economy of Athens while women's central function was to breed pure Athenian citizens. The latter remained under male guardianship and were supposed to get married at an early age in order to devote themselves to their families. Their duties were confined to household activities, as well as the performance of religious rituals, and their expectations and roles are clearly reflected in *Antigone*.

The performance

The theatrical space

Antigone was first performed in the morning in the open-air Theatre of Dionysus, on the south-east slope of the Acropolis, just above the temple of Dionysus and close (on the other side of the Acropolis hill) to the market-place (*agora*) where all political, judicial, commercial and religious activities took place, making it both metaphorically and literally the centre of the city.

The shape of the theatre itself developed according to the topography of the Acropolis hill. This meant that the hillside rising up from the temple of Dionysus gradually formed a natural theatre auditorium with the audience sitting initially on the ground and later on wooden planks. This offered spectators a better view than level ground, allowing them to look down on a performance area (*orchestra*) which gradually developed into a circle where the tragedies unfolded through the skilful acting and dancing of the performers.

A wooden structure, the stage building or *skene*, was positioned on the circular performance area. The front of the *skene* was dominated by a central door, marking the boundary between inner and outer space, private and public domain, and to a certain degree between female and male spheres. At a practical level it also served as the place where actors changed costumes and masks without being seen. The invention of *skenographia* (scene painting) is credited by Aristotle to Sophocles. The front of the *skene* was probably rendered to look like a palace, temple, etc., depending on the play's context.

Apart from the central door, the circular performance area had another two side-entrances from which the male characters usually arrived or departed. Women, in contrast, usually used the main door, with the exception of Antigone, who is no ordinary female. She departs boldly by the side-entrance to bury her brother and she is later brought back from the same direction as a captive. When Creon arrests both sisters they are taken 'inside' where they belong, through the central door, from which Antigone will soon after make her final journey to meet her death.

Finally, due to the open-air nature of the theatre it was impossible for the spectators to observe the play without taking into account their surroundings, including the temple of Dionysus, the Parthenon (temple of Athene) looming just behind them, the market on the other side of the slope, the rocky terrain, the city walls, the sea and sunny sky, which would have served as natural correlatives to the performer's words and actions. Equally, the entrances and exits would have been arranged to draw meaning from the topography of the theatre, with each side giving a different feel to the spectators. In most tragedies the right side is connected with the civilised and ordered world of the city and the left with the wilderness of the country.

The actors

In ancient Greek theatre three professional male actors, the protagonist (first competitor), deuteragonist (second competitor) and tritagonist (third competitor), interpreted all the characters in the play, their status depending on the length and difficulty of their roles. The actors were assigned to the dramatist by the state official in charge of the festival, but on many occasions, the poet himself could also participate by playing the central part. It is important to note that the poet was not a simple dramatist but also functioned as the modern-day director, guiding and instructing his actors on how to perform their parts. According to Aristotle, Sophocles was the first dramatist to make use of a third speaker. However Aeschylus' *Oresteia* shows evidence of a third actor with Pylades in *Choephoroi*, who delivers a single line.

There have been various suggestions concerning the distribution of parts in *Antigone*. It is obvious that when two characters co-existed on stage the parts could not be interpreted by the same actor. With this in mind the most likely distribution would seem to be the following: the role of Creon would have been played by the protagonist since his part is longest and he appears on stage with all the other characters; the second actor would have interpreted Antigone, Haemon, Teiresias and Eurydice, while the third actor would have played the smaller and less significant roles of Ismene, the soldier and the messenger. In practice this would have been an interesting distribution since all the opponents of Creon would have shared the same voice and attitude, while the third actor would have delivered the parts of those who represented a more moderate and ordinary mentality.

Another interesting interpretation suggests that, rather than the protagonist being allotted a single role, the most demanding and challenging sections were distributed to the most talented and experienced performer. In this case, the protagonist would have initially interpreted the role of Antigone and after her death would have interpreted the role of Creon. This approach leans more on the necessity of skills when interpreting difficult and intense dramatic moments to produce a theatrically unifying quality to the production, and less on the modern Stanislavskian conception of the actor's need to interpret a single dramatic part in order to establish a psychological and intellectual connection with the character as it develops throughout the play. The characters are seen as physical entities that are complete only when realised in performance and not as dramatic entities that pre-exist in the words of the text.

As the content of the play suggests, the spectators would have witnessed a series of simple but well-constructed confrontations between two actors, but no special effects were required. In contrast, it was the power of masked acting, the configuration of the parts of the body, and one actor in relation to another or to the chorus, as well as the effectiveness of the speech, as that dictated meaning and produced a sense of excitement. During the performance, the spectators looked down on three masked actors who wore long colourful robes (*chiton*), spoke clearly and moved in a stylised manner highlighting the ceremonial quality of the production. The use of masks naturally facilitated the swift changes from one part to another, while at the same time helping to identify the gender and age of each character, especially for those viewing from a distance. For example, female masks were paler than male since women had lighter skins because they spent most of their time indoors, while older males were distinguished from young boys by facial hair.

Beyond these practical reasons, however, it is important to underline that in ancient Greece the use of the mask was not an exotic concept but a natural way of performing and its presence was perceived as a defining element of theatre, representing the loss of the actor's persona to the persona of the mythical character. Moreover, it determined the overall acting technique, as the movements and gestures of the performers required to be enhanced to make up for the lack of facial expression. The notion of psychological acting through the subtle variations of facial expression was alien to the ancient Greeks. Speech also became an important component of the performance as the masked and fully covered bodies naturally drove the audience's attention to the spoken words, which in conjunction with the formal figures and their spatial context produced theatrical meaning. Equally important to the direction of meaning was the presence and movement of the chorus with its various functions.

The chorus

The members of the chorus were selected by the Athenian community of citizens six to eight months in advance in order to start their demanding training. Although amateurs, they would still have been extremely skilful, due to their familiarity with and participation in other dances that were part of most ritual events of the city.

During the performance of *Antigone* the members of the chorus abandoned their individuality to become a group of fifteen masked male dancers dressed in long robes. (Sophocles increased the number of the tragic chorus from twelve to fifteen.) These dancers represented a single organism which projected a single voice, the voice of the elders of Thebes.

The members of the chorus, with the accompaniment of the double-pipe player, were required to dance and sing in unison the lyrics of the play with clear articulation and precise movements, highlighting visually and verbally the events and words that were played out before them. The rhythm of the words must have guided their movements, while the various metres in which the lyrics were written must have assumed particular dance steps that pointed to familiar ritual practices, making them easily recognisable to the spectators. Thus, the choreography of the group was an essential component of the experience, producing theatrical meaning through dance. As Rush Rehm suggests:

> The precise nature of the dance of the chorus has been lost but we gain some insight from the content and substance of the songs, from representations of dancers on ancient vases and sculpture, and from the lyric metres themselves. It seems likely that the Greek chorus did not eschew mimetic and expressive movements. When they sang of the animal world and the forces of nature, there was a quality in the dance that reflected its power and beauty. When the lyric included threnodic elements and other aspects of mourning rites, or dealt with sacrifice, weddings, athletic contests, or military actions, we may be sure the dance drew on recognisable gestures and movements from those rituals and events. (Rehm, 1992, p. 54)

It is difficult to guess the exact formations that the chorus developed on stage but one can assume that the odd number of fifteen would have encouraged a split into sub-groups and would have generated a strategic position for the chorus leader whose key responsibility was to guide his fellow dancers.

The chorus's attitude would not necessarily have been that of Sophocles or the attitude he wished to instil in his audience, but their position between actors and audience gave them part of the nature of both. They might have commented or reflected on the confrontations of characters such as Ismene and Antigone, the soldier and Creon, Creon and Antigone, Haemon and Creon, Creon and Teiresias, by division into semi-choruses and by corporate response to each speaker in turn, and it is highly unlikely that they would have stood and watched impassively. It is agreed by most practitioners and spectators, who have viewed the revival of an ancient chorus on stage, that their physical movements, far from detracting from the focus of attention, can actually confirm it. Moreover in large open-air theatres such as the ancient Greek ones, the further away the audience sits, the greater the effect.

In conclusion, the theatrical purpose of the chorus could be understood in many ways but one of its most important functions was its ability to enhance the audience's understanding of the play through their physical reactions to the actions and words of the central characters. The ever-present chorus could function as a second audience that, due to its closeness to the events and its strategic position between characters and spectators, was powerful enough to guide the latter on how to appreciate the various dramatic situations.

Interpretations of *Antigone*

One can never be sure of the original intentions of a play written to be staged two and a half thousand years ago or the way in which the original audience perceived the scenes and the tragedy as a whole. Such considerations will always remain speculative. Equally it is inevitable that the tragedy will yield different meanings for spectators today according to the context in which it is presented, or in the case of readers, the context of their study. However most critics agree that some interpretations and approaches are more convincing than others.

The principal 'meaning' is obviously generated by the opposition between Antigone and Creon. The German philosopher Hegel used this state of conflict to explain the tragedy and at the same time project his own philosophical views of dialectics.[1] His influential theory is based on his reading of the play in terms of opposing principles (family versus state) which ultimately lead to the destruction of the two individuals. According to him, both characters are right in principle but are unable to see the limited validity of their claims, which results in their tragic endings. Hegel also argues that the central idea of conflict leads to a final synthesis, which ensures a better future for the survivors who have become more insightful through the course of the tragedy. The final lines of the chorus state exactly this:

> Today it has happened here. With our own eyes
> We have seen an old man, through suffering, become wise.

Even though many critics have argued that by reading the play purely as a set of oppositions we run the risk of reducing the protagonists to one-dimensional representatives of simple antithetical principles, thus oversimplifying the play and

[1] For Hegel's treatment of the play see Hegel, *On Tragedy*.

misunderstanding Sophocles' sense of the tragic, it remains indisputable that both characters are the focus of the play, producing a 'double centre of gravity' and creating a tension which makes the action more rich and complex.

The essence of this complexity lies not so much in the characters themselves as in the bond which links one to the other. Neither can exist without the other and in the same way the issues they represent cannot be fully appreciated without the tension produced by their simultaneous existence. As C. H. Whitman has remarked, 'Antigone is the balance in which Creon is weighed, and found wanting'; on the other hand, Antigone's harshness would make no sense without Creon's authoritarian wilfulness.[1]

The issues embodied through the presence of the two protagonists have been conceptualised in many ways, some of the most important being politics (family versus state), gender (female versus male), justice and religion (divine law versus human law). One must acknowledge, however, that the characters are also individuals with certain emotions and characteristics, involved in a number of complex situations and circumstances. Their human distinctiveness gives the themes substance and life, even more so when presented on stage.

The characters

It is impossible to evaluate a character from Greek tragedy in purely psychological terms since Athenian drama does not offer the same details and depth of characterisation to be found in the plays of, for example, Ibsen. The internal psychological states remain largely unformulated by the text. Even though Sophocles' characters achieve a degree of coherence and distinctiveness that encourages the spectator or reader to begin to respond to them as if they were real persons, their essential qualities and characteristics derive either from their typical heroic status or seem defined by their precise social roles.

[1] Whitman, 1951, p. 86. For more on the bond which links Antigone and Creon, see Segal, 'Sophocles' Praise of Man and the Conflicts of the *Antigone*', in Woodard, 1966, pp. 46–66.

The central characters and the idea of the Sophoclean hero/heroine

All of Sophocles' dramas portray an important central character around whom the tragedy unfolds and who could be described as isolated, set apart from his/her 'normal' fellow humans. In *Antigone* the central characters are two, Antigone and Creon, and the entire action comes as a result of the clash between these very powerful and dynamic personalities. Their characteristics match those of the Sophoclean hero as described by the critic B. M. W. Knox in his famous study of *The Heroic Temper*.

According to Knox, the Sophoclean hero is a character who, in the face of human opposition, makes a decision which derives from his individual nature, and then passionately maintains that decision even to the point of self-destruction. The hero decides against compromise as he refuses to yield; remains true to himself and his 'nature', which he inherited from his parents and which is his identity. Thus the heroic qualities include stubbornness, outspokenness and above all courage.

In *Antigone* it is clear that the heroine is faced with opposition from Ismene's urgent appeals, the threats of her uncle Creon and the strong disapproval of the chorus. Although Creon maintains his confident expectation that Antigone's defiant mood will be subdued, he is proved wrong as she goes to her death undefeated like a true Sophoclean heroine. She holds firm against the massive pressure of society, of friends as well as enemies. Antigone is stubborn, self-willed, insisting throughout the play on her own way and on her rightness.

Creon, on the other hand, seems at first sight to be the true hero of the play as he is presented, like the Aristotelian tragic hero,[1] as a man of authority who comes crashing down from his position of greatness. But he lacks the heroic temperament. In Creon we are presented with a man who displays every symptom of heroic stubbornness but who in the end is swayed by advice, makes major concessions until his final collapse. He fails to live up to his principles and his great personality, which is nothing but a false persona.

[1] The true tragic hero, according to Aristotle (*c.* 336 BC), is a man of power whose situation, by the end of the play, is reversed, 'a person who is neither perfect in virtue or justice, nor one who falls into misfortune through vice and depravity, but rather, one who succumbs through some miscalculation (*hamartia*)' (Aristotle, *Poetics* 13, trans. Leon Golden, New Jersey, Prentice Hall, 1967).

So as the play unfolds it gradually becomes clear that the natures of the two characters are different, with Antigone remaining loyal to her convictions and Creon belatedly trying to avoid destruction by accepting responsibility for his mistaken conduct. One could argue that while two characters assume the heroic attitude in this tragedy only one of them in the end is exposed as heroic, Antigone.[1] However, as Knox observes, the clash between Antigone and Creon is much more than a confrontation between the true hero and the false. The conflict raises political and religious questions of the highest importance, which will be discussed later.

The supporting or 'lesser' characters

Antigone's and Creon's powerful personalities are not only realised through their direct confrontations with each other but also through their contrast with other less important and more 'normal' community members. The continuous presentation of conflicting personalities and principles fuels the tragedy's series of confrontations.

Out of all the lesser characters only Haemon could be described as coming close to the heroic nature of Antigone. In his attempt to defend his fiancée to his father he exposes his passionate, uncompromising and emotional nature while at the same time underlining Creon's isolation and mistaken conduct. At a lower level, he, like Antigone, resolves to die and he is the only one who comes close to understanding her. In his final act he is indeed 'married' to her in death, while the way in which his strong romantic feelings for Antigone guides his words and his actions is typical. Haemon's strong feelings have led many to interpret the play as a love story.

Ismene in contrast to Haemon appears as the voice of reason while her mild and submissive nature is characteristic of her position in Theban (Athenian) society, an unmarried woman under the authority of male guardianship. She is necessary to highlight the unorthodox behaviour and extreme nature of Antigone. Her position is clear: she shares Antigone's feelings for the family, but yields to superior force. Her conduct is much closer to what the

[1] For more on the debate about who is the true 'hero' or protagonist of the play, who dominates the action, whose suffering is the primary subject, see James C. Hogan, 'The protagonists of Antigone', *Arethusa*, 5, 1972, pp. 93–100.

Athenians expected of their women than her sister's bold defiance of her male ruler.

The remaining characters have some personal characteristics to make them credible human beings but more essentially they contribute to the meaning of the play by instigating a series of reactions from the central characters, encouraging the spectators to appreciate the protagonists' natures and principles in a more rounded way. The prophet Teiresias is typical. He represents the divine powers and underlines that there are realms of existence that man should not seek to control. It is through his presence that Creon's disrespect for the gods is fully made clear and from his intervention Creon's decision to reconsider his position begins.

The chorus

There have been plenty of discussions about whether the chorus plays an active role or is merely a passive commentator on the action. In any case, it is undisputed that Sophocles did integrate the chorus more fully into his dramas than his predecessor Aeschylus.

The chorus in *Antigone* is made up of Theban elders concerned, as is Creon, with the good of the state. Like the soldier, the chorus avoid taking a firm position and only on a very few occasions do they indicate on whose side they might stand, Antigone's or Creon's. Their reaction to Creon's decision is muted, typical of their moderate attitude. They acknowledge the king's power and authority and have no desire to dispute his decision by disobeying him. Only when the Theban elders realise that Creon doubts his own decision, after listening to Teiresias's warnings, do they at last take a stand and call on him to yield.

As far as their relationship with the heroine is concerned, the chorus show little sympathy for Antigone whom they consider both wild in nature and doomed by the curse of her family. There have been various suggestions concerning the chorus's negative attitude to Antigone. Some of the most significant are (a) that the chorus is afraid of the ever-present Creon and thus avoids expressing their honest positive opinions; (b) their gender and age automatically distance them from the young, passionate female, placing them on Creon's side of civic law and male order; (c) it highlights the isolation of the central character, emphasising her heroic status. All three reasons could be projected on stage in very interesting and visually effective ways through positioning a group of people against a single actor.

Finally the chorus's odes, which clearly belong in a different register, deal mainly with general issues with some relevance to the play, which might indirectly have some bearing on the specific situation. In these sections the chorus maintains its more traditional role of dancing and singing of mythological subjects and poetic themes full of rich imagery.

Central themes

The central characters of the play appear to represent a number of issues connected with ideas about politics, gender, justice and religion. The relationship, however, between the character and a particular issue is not always as simple and straightforward as it initially appears. Neither of the characters is entirely consistent in word or practice. For example, even though Creon might initially be perceived as the representative of democratic rule, giving speeches about democratic loyalty and equality before the law, his actions and attitude during the course of the play prove that he could also become an oppressive tyrant demanding obedience, right or wrong, from his subjects. In the same way, the characteristics of Antigone as a female (dedication to family) could be questioned since her behaviour suggests a venture into the male sphere of public action. Thus the issue of gender (female versus male) becomes rather complex.

With this in mind, I shall discuss a number of central themes present in the play and expressed through the opposition of the characters as well as through their contradictory natures.

Politics (family versus state)

The action of the play, as in most Greek tragedies, unfolds in front of a palace where, besides the members of the royal family, a number of figures including the chorus come to attend the needs of the family, consult and sympathise with them. The distinction between the royal few and the anonymous citizens is made clear in that the latter act as passive spectators to the tragedy which is taking place between the residents of the palace. Without the actions of the royal family there would be no tragedy.

In the course of the play the real audience (external audience), along with the chorus, messenger and soldier (internal audience), witness a number of conflicts, the most important occurring between a ruler who expresses his loyalty to the state and his young niece who openly disregards the state and declares her dedication to her father's family and the ties of kinship. The development of the play sees Creon turning into an authoritarian figure and the young girl dying for her convictions as a true heroine who refuses to yield. The closure of the play is not very clear but some commentators (Hegel) have suggested that it is positive because it offers signs of a more harmonious political future between ruler and citizens with Creon reconsidering and eventually changing his initial harmful attitude.

The restoration of democracy and order does not, however, seem to occur through any kind of democratic procedure but rather through Antigone's courageous defiance, Haemon's strong love for his cousin and the indirect intervention of the gods in the person of Teiresias. Thus the anonymous citizens do little to resolve the crisis and so confirm their unheroic status and non-exceptional nature. This could be read as a political statement which suggests that family and divine powers (the curse of the family has been sent by the gods) are the solution as much as the problem in this tragic conflict, while the community fulfils the role of passive spectator.

As well as the political situation of the play, we have indirect references to the current political situation in Athens. The conflict between state and family as expressed through the clash between Creon and Antigone was very clearly defined in fifth-century Athens and would easily have been identified by the spectators in their own lives (see pp. xix–xxi). Initially Creon acts as a good political leader, like Pericles, favouring the state above family kinship. Consequently Polynices, no matter what his relationship to Creon, must be treated as an enemy of the state. Excessive power, however, turns the king into a bad leader and this could have been perceived by fifth-century spectators as a warning against democratic rulers who abuse their position of authority.

Antigone, in contrast, cannot ignore her ties with her brother and chooses to die for him in spite of his actions against the city. The traditional claims of family ties was a very familiar issue to the Athenians who in the character of Antigone would have recalled the old values which flourished when the central political institution had been the extended family.

Gender (male versus female)

Gender is a key issue in *Antigone*, determining in many ways the actions of the central characters. Throughout the play the role of women, the possibility of female independent thinking and decision-making as well as their subjection to male authority, are questioned causing much discussion and opposing interpretations of the play.

As already mentioned, a young Athenian woman's social acceptance came through marriage and children (see p. xxi). After she got married she was supposed to remain loyal to her new and her old family, father and brother as well as husband and son. The subordination of the wife to the husband, female to male, was not only a determining factor in the definition of citizenship in Athens but also a fundamental element of the order of the household. Antigone as an unmarried girl is still attached to her father's family and she refuses the prospect of attachment to any other group. She places a brother above a son ('Not even for a son would I have done this', p. 39). Even though her defiance of Creon and death might be admirable, the sacrifice of marriage and children would have seemed perverse.

The figure of Antigone is curiously ambiguous and conflicted in gender. In the course of the play she follows traditional female social roles through her insistence on honouring her family and performing the burial rites for her brother, voicing the claims of kin and the cult of the dead. Yet her attitude and outspoken manner, in contrast to the conventional feminine mentality of Ismene, highlight her inner drive to act as a non-ordinary woman. Thus, while the authoritarian status of men is quite clear in the play through the words and actions of Creon, what should be expected of women is open to a number of questions.

Recently feminist critics have argued that the heroine, by acting against her sister's advice and Creon's decree, assumes an essentially masculine role.[1] Others however argue that Antigone does not act unconventionally in defying Creon because he is violating established custom (in fifth century BC, it was obligatory to bury family members), and that by demanding obedience to his will, he is misusing his power as a ruler, behaving like a tyrant. Far from being unconventional, Antigone is only doing what her family

[1] H. Foley, 'The Conception of Women in Athenian Drama' in Foley, 1981, pp. 127–67.

might have expected of her as a woman.[1] But what is the final outcome? Is it the male authority of Creon or the wild irrational female nature of Antigone that prevails?

The answer depends on whom we view as the true hero. Antigone, on the one hand, could be seen as being destroyed by her venture into the male sphere of public action, while her conventional and moderate sister who has not disrupted male order survives into safe invisibility and silence. Conversely, we could view Antigone as the female heroine who, through her death, has shown incredible strength and commitment to her true family while exposing the mistaken conduct and abusive nature of Creon. Like other women in epic and drama, Antigone wins praise for acting on behalf of her family. In contrast, Creon is horribly punished by seeing the death of his family, and having his convictions and self-esteem shattered.

In any case, Antigone remains one of the most impressive and complex female stage characters in refusing to yield to Creon's male authority and an unfair political system made by men.

Justice (divine versus human law)

Through the characters of Antigone and Creon the play also shows a city in which civic laws are divided from divine justice. The position of Creon is typical in this, declaring in his initial speeches that the most important law is that of the state and warning his people that if they disobey his decree and bury Polynices' corpse they will be punished accordingly.

> . . . Crimes
> Against the State and its laws, you'll find,
> Are very unprofitable in the end. (p. 16)

Antigone in contrast believes in a different legal system in which family and kinship ties are valued and an unburied corpse means pollution and demonstrates disrespect for the gods of the underworld. In her famous speech justifying her actions in burying her brother, she invokes 'the law of god'. Natural justice is the reason for disobeying her uncle. These laws, as she describes them in the same speech,

[1] M. Lefkowitz, *Women in Greek Myth*, London, Duckworth, 1986.

are not written down, and never change.
They are for today, yesterday and all time.
No one understands where they come from,
But everyone recognises their force:
And no man's arrogance or power
Can make me disobey them. (pp. 21–2)

She introduces for the first time the distinction between artificial law ('decree') and natural law ('law') which up to this point had been used indiscriminately by Creon. From now on justice in private life can no longer be identified with justice in relation to the polis or state. Antigone by challenging human law and standing outside the state definition of justice pays the price of losing her life, but at the end it is Creon who faces total destruction. After Teiresias' intervention and witnessing his son's and his wife's deaths, Creon admits that by disregarding divine rules and disallowing the burial of Polynices, he has been punished and therefore accepts full responsibility for his disrespectful actions. 'All the guilt is mine!' he says.

The chorus's final assessment reaffirms the general principle that divine law will always overrule human justice:

The key to human happiness
Is to nurture wisdom in your heart,
For man to attend to man's business
And let the gods play their part:
Above all, to stand in awe
Of the eternal, unalterable law.
The proud man may pretend
In his arrogance to despise
Everything but himself. In the end
The gods will bring him to grief.
Today it has happened here. With our own eyes
We have seen an old man, through suffering , become wise. (p. 55)

For this reason many commentators believe that the issue of justice and religion is one of the key themes of the play, used by Sophocles to give a religious lesson to those who full of 'pride and arrogance' disregard traditional divine rules and customs and forget that civic law must be part of natural law.

Modern reception of *Antigone*

Even as you read this section there is a production of *Antigone* being mounted somewhere around the world. A vast number of interpretations are continually being expressed, through adaptation of the original text or in the presentation of the tragedy on stage. As George Steiner points out, 'Each production of Sophocles' *Antigone* since the first is a dynamic enactment of understanding.'[1]

The number of these productions makes the task of covering the entire modern reception of *Antigone* impossible. For this reason I have chosen to focus on a few of the most significant, significant either because they have added something to traditional interpretations or because they have broken a past tradition and discovered an entirely new dimension for the play.

Antigone *in the nineteenth century*

The philosopher Hegel, with his influential theory on *Antigone*, was a key figure in making the tragedy popular in the nineteenth century. His reading of the play as a moral lesson through which people could become wiser by appreciating the relationship between moral goodness and political success, between human achievement and divine approval, was a very appealing interpretation in those days of political liberalism. The tragedy was chosen by the Prussian king Friedrich Wilhelm IV because, through the moderate voice of the chorus representing the city, it became the perfect illustration of the idea of the 'moral community' as expressed through the new liberalism of the time.

The production that secured the popularity of *Antigone* for years to come opened at the Hoftheater in Potsdam in October 1841 and became known as the 'Mendelssohn *Antigone*'. This sobriquet was chosen because the choral introduction and music for the lyrics were composed by Felix Mendelssohn. The translation by Johann Jakob Christian Donner was metrically complex, trying to keep as faithful as possible to the original text, and the responsibility for the staging was largely given to the famous director Ludwig Tieck who tried to avoid the use of special effects and illusionist techniques in favour of a simpler 'authentic' setting. After this production, the play was presented in different countries not necessarily with the intention of sending a political message. It was

[1] Steiner, 1984, p. 198.

rather the authenticity of the staging and costumes as well as the impressive mixture of song and speech in tragedy that appealed to nineteenth-century audiences in England, France, Russia and the newly liberated modern Greece.

Adaptations of Antigone *in the twentieth century*

In the twentieth century most productions and adaptations of *Antigone* have been interested in finding different ways to express how the individual relates to the state. Their main goal has been to highlight the political message of the play, this time not as a moral lesson to political leaders, but rather as an example of firm resistance to authoritarian regimes. This is not to say that all productions shared the same political intentions.

Anouilh's adaptation, for example, far from giving a lesson on how to resist oppressive states, demonstrates the futility of active political engagement. It caused a great deal of controversy when first performed in 1944 because of its favourable portrayal of Creon in the political climate of the time (Nazi-occupied France). In Anouilh's play whether Antigone or Creon is right is ambiguous, but it is almost certain that Creon is not wrong. Creon is portrayed as an emergency political leader who has a duty to keep the city in order and for this noble cause he gives up everything that is precious to him. Antigone on the other hand is a romantic young girl who causes trouble and anarchy in her attempt to fulfil her thirst for a world of purity. At the end Creon wins the intellectual argument and Antigone chooses to die in her attempt to defy the values of bourgeois society. This reading of the play secured its presentation in Nazi-occupied France and produced a number of faithful fans among the bourgeois society, who could relate to the characters. It also caused a great degree of hostility from the French left. The latter considered the play an apologia for the French collaborators in power.[1]

Another famous adaptation of the play, which, unlike Anouilh's 'boulevard' version, sent a strong political message against the German fascist regime, was Brecht's *Antigone*. His version, in contrast to other adaptations of the time, gave the chorus a central position in the play, allowing the audience to consider its political

[1] For more on the controversial production and other performances, see Ted Freeman's very informative introduction to Anouilh's *Antigone* in the Methuen Student Edition of the play (1988).

message and theatrical function. The Theban elders were no longer 'a moral community' as perceived by Hegel, but represented the German majority who, no matter their disapproval of the fascist regime, were unable to rebel against it. Brecht's chorus is passive and although they try to distance themselves from Creon prove incapable of breaking free from his authority. In the production, which was set in a remote 'half-oriental antiquity', the four actors who comprised the chorus wore identical clothes to Creon, shared the same performance space and spoke in a similar manner, highlighting in this way their adherence to him. Their theatrical function was to retain a sentimental distance between Antigone and the audience. This was achieved through their bodily language (*Gestus*), which commented on the heroine's actions, preventing an emotional bond from developing with the spectators and producing an intellectual and sentimental detachment. As Brecht stated, when the actress played for sympathy it ran the risk of obscuring 'the audience's vision of the root conflict within the ruling class'. Brecht's political version of the play, with the help of the chorus, allowed both audience and actors to listen carefully to the arguments and decide on the rightness of each side.

In 1967 the Living Theatre Company of Julian Beck and Judith Malina used Brecht's adaptation to express a different set of objectives. This time the play's message became connected to the liberation of the individual from his own self guilt. The production highlighted the current political concerns about the Vietnam War as well as the ideological stance of the sixties' 'flower children'. All the actors wore jeans which brought the play into contemporary New York and the audience was given an active role by becoming the invading army from Argos. The insistence on including the audience within the performance was a characteristic of the experimental theatre of the sixties, highly influenced by Grotowski's ideas on the performer/spectator bond. The performance was also clearly influenced by Artaud's ideal of 'total theatre' where mind and body, words and actions cannot be separated on stage. For this reason, during the production all words were translated into actions, creating a succession of fluid group images, for example, a number of bodies representing the sea, or the projection of Creon's emotions through various formations of the chorus's bodies on stage. The performance looked inwards and was concerned with the self and the ways in which people perceived and interpreted visual images. The key message of the production, as expressed through Malina's Antigone, was that reason, when separated from feelings and instincts, is insufficient to resolve any kind of tragic conflict and that those who follow their emotions are in the end the true heroes.

The twentieth-century Antigone has often been viewed as a character who resists the oppression of the state in a heroic manner, providing an inspiring example of mental resistance against tyrannical governments. A famous example of this is Athol Fugard's reconstruction of the Antigone story in his play *The Island* (1972). It was inspired by a production of *Antigone* that was staged in a prison with Nelson Mandela as Antigone. The story which fuses real-life and fictional events develops as follows: Two prisoners, John who is about to be released from prison, and Winston who has been sentenced by the regime to life imprisonment, improvise a two-man production of *Antigone* with the prisoners as the audience. John plays Creon and Winston plays Antigone. The final scene of the improvised play is 'The Trial and Punishment of Antigone' during which Winston pleads guilty but at the same time declares his belief in a higher law. After his life sentence has been announced, Winston takes off the clothes that helped him impersonate Antigone and speaks in his own character, announcing that he is going to his living death because he honoured those things that deserved his honour. Winston, just like the mythical character he impersonated, goes undefeated to serve his life sentence.

Finally, I would like to mention the 1986 BBC televised version of *Antigone* as an attempt to introduce Greek drama to a vast and diverse audience without making it 'boring and out of date'. The production aimed to make the play convincing and pleasurable for all those scholars 'who have spent a life studying the texts' but at the same time a thrilling experience for those who had never before heard of Greek drama. The version once again highlighted the oppressive nature of Creon and the heroic resistance of Antigone, adding a clear political tone to the play and making it relevant to the Cold War politics and other current political events of the eighties. As Don Taylor remarks when discussing the political relevance of the Sophocles' play to contemporary events during his BBC rehearsals,

> Nothing could have illustrated that more clearly than the fact that we were rehearsing the *Antigone* during the summer of 1984, in the first

> months of the miners' strike, and throughout the drama of the Sarah Tisdall trial. In both cases, the words being spoken in our rehearsal-room exactly paralleled the arguments being rehearsed in the papers and on the TV political discussion programmes. (Translator's Introduction, *Sophocles: Plays One*, p. lix)

The nature of the translation, as one will observe when reading this volume, reflects the fact that it was made for TV and for this reason had to exclude or at least keep to the minimum the poetic quality of the words spoken by Sophocles' characters. Don Taylor admitted that it was impossible to use any existing translation of the time, however effective, in television. Television by nature demanded a more lively language. As he stated,

> Though television is a good medium for genuine dramatic poetry it is merciless with any kind of stilted language, and it soon became clear to us that we could present none of the existing translations of the Sophoclean trilogy with the faintest chance of the particular kind of success we hoped for. (Translator's Note, p. xlix)

Don Taylor's translation suited the production and fulfilled his aim of making a popular version that seemed to have been written 'not 2,500 years ago, but the day before yesterday, today and tomorrow'.

From these diverse examples of adaptations and revivals it is obvious that the ancient Greek tragedies will never be exhausted provided that artists and audiences use their creativity and enthusiasm to discover and yield their potential meanings.[1]

[1] For more on the adaptations and revivals mentioned in this section, see P. Burian, 'Tragedy Adapted for Stages and Screens: the Renaissance to the Present', pp. 253, 283, F. Macintosh, 'Tragedy in Performance: Nineteenth and Twentieth-century Productions', in Easterling, 1997, pp. 284–8, and Wiles, 2000, pp. 62–5.

Further Reading

The Greek text

Sophoclis Fabulae, ed. H. Lloyd-Jones and N. G. Wilson, Oxford, OUP, 1990 (Greek text only)

Sophocles, ed. and trans. H. Lloyd-Jones, 3 vols, Cambridge MA, Harvard University Press (Greek text, facing English translation, introduction and notes)

Antigone, ed. Mark Griffith, Cambridge, CUP, 1999 (Greek text, very useful and informative introduction and notes)

Selected translations of Sophocles in English

Sophocles: Plays One, Methuen, London, 1986 (includes *Oedipus the King*, *Oedipus at Colonus*, *Antigone*)

Sophocles: Plays Two, Methuen, London, 1990 (includes *Ajax*, *Women of Trachis*, *Electra*, *Philoctetes*)

Sophocles: 'Antigone', 'Oedipus' and 'Electra', trans. H. D. F. Kitto, Oxford, OUP, 1998

Sophocles: The Three Theban Plays, trans. R. Fagles, Harmondsworth, Penguin, 1984

Greek theatre and drama

Allan, A. and Storey, Ian C. (eds), *A Guide to Ancient Greek Drama,* Oxford, Blackwell, 2004

Arnott, P. D., *Public and Performance in the Greek Theatre,* London, Routledge, 1989

Aylen, Leo, *The Greek Theatre,* New Jersey, Associated University Press, 1985

Bieber, M., *The Greek and Roman Theatre,* Princeton, Princeton University Press, 1961

Csapo, E. and Slater, W. J., *The Context of Ancient Drama,* Ann Arbor, University of Michigan Press, 1995

Easterling, P. E. (ed.), *Cambridge Companion to Greek Tragedy*, Cambridge, CUP, 1997
Foley, H., 'The Conception of Women in Athenian Drama' in H. Foley (ed.), *Reflections of Women in Antiquity*, New York, Gordon and Breach, 1981
Green, J. R., *Theatre in Ancient Greek Society*, London, Routledge, 1994
Green, J. R and Handley, E., *Images of the Greek Theatre*, London, British Museum Press, 1995
Knox, Bernard (ed.), *Word and Action: Essays on the Ancient Theatre*, Baltimore, Johns Hopkins University Press, 1979
Ley, G., *A Short Introduction to the Greek Theatre*, Chicago, University of Chicago Press, 1991
Pickard-Cambridge, A., *The Dramatic Festivals of Athens*, 2nd ed. revised J. Gould and D. M. Lewis, Oxford, OUP, 1968
Rehm, Rush, *Greek Tragic Theatre*, London, Routledge, 1992
Taplin, Oliver, *Greek Tragedy in Action*, London, Methuen, 1978
——, *The Stagecraft of Aeschylus: The Dramatic Use of Exits and Entrances in Greek Tragedy*, Oxford, Clarendon Press, 1977
Walcot, Peter, *Greek Drama in its Theatrical and Social Context*, Cardiff, University of Wales Press, 1976
Walton, J. Michael, *Greek Theatre Practice*, London, Methuen, 1980
——, *The Greek Sense of Theatre*, London, Methuen, 1984
——, *Living Greek Theatre: A Handbook of Classical Performance and Modern Production*, Westport, Greenwood Press, 1988
Wiles, David, *Tragedy in Athens*, Cambridge, CUP, 1997
——, *Greek Theatre Performance: An Introduction*, Cambridge, CUP, 2000

General studies of Sophocles

Bloom, H., *Sophocles*, New York, Chelsea House, 1990
Blundell, M. W., *Helping Friends and Harming Enemies: A Study in Sophocles and Greek Ethics*, Cambridge, CUP, 1989
Burton, R. W. B., *The Chorus in Sophocles' Tragedies*, Oxford, OUP, 1980
Buxton, R. G., *Sophocles*, Oxford, OUP, 1984
Gardiner, C.P., *The Sophoclean Chorus*, Iowa City, University of Iowa Press, 1987

Gellie, G. H., *Sophocles*, Melbourne, Melbourne University Press, 1972
Kirkwood, G. M., *A Study of Sophoclean Drama*, Ithaca, Cornell University Press, 1958; 2nd ed. 1994
Kitto, H. D. F., *Sophocles: Dramatist and Philosopher,* London, Greenwood Press, 1958
Knox, B. M. W., *The Heroic Temper*, Berkeley and Los Angeles, University of California Press, 1964
Seale, D., *Vision and Stagecraft in Sophocles*, London, Croom Helm, 1982
Segal, C. P., *Sophocles' Tragic World: Divinity, Nature, Society*, Cambridge MA, Harvard University Press, 1995
——, *Tragedy and Civilization: An Interpretation of Sophocles,* Cambridge, CUP, 1981
Waldock, A. J. A., *Sophocles the Dramatist*, Cambridge, CUP, 1951
Webster, T. B. L., *An Introduction to Sophocles*, 2nd ed., London, Methuen, 1969
Whitman, C. H., *Sophocles*: *A study of Heroic Humanism,* Cambridge MA, Harvard University Press, 1951
Winnington-Ingram, R. P., *Sophocles*, Cambridge, CUP, 1980
Woodard, T. (ed.), *Sophocles: A Collection of Critical Essays*, Englewood Cliffs, NJ, Prentice Hall, 1966

Studies and articles on *Antigone*

Brown, A. L. (ed.), *Sophocles: 'Antigone',* Warminster, Aris and Phillips, 1987
Calder, W. M., 'Sophocles' Political Tragedy: *Antigone*', *Greek Roman and Byzantine Studies*, ix, 1968, pp. 389–407
——, 'The Protagonist of Sophocles' *Antigone*', *Arethusa*, iv, 1971, pp. 49–52
Crane, G., 'Creon and the "Ode to Man" in Sophocles' *Antigone*', *Harvard Studies in Classical Philology*, 92, 1989, pp. 103–16
Easterling, P. E., 'Character in Sophocles', *Greece and Rome*, 24, 1977, pp. 121–9
——, 'The Second Stasimon of Sophocles' *Antigone*' in R. D. Dawe, J. Diggle and P. E. Easterling (eds), *Dionysiaca*, Cambridge, CUP, 1978, pp. 141–58
Goheen, R. F., *The Imagery of Sophocles'* 'Antigone', Princeton,

Princeton University Press, 1951

Hamilton, J. D. B., '*Antigone*: Kinship, Justice, and the Polis', in D. C. Pozzi and J. M. Wickersham (eds), *Myth and the Polis*, Ithaca, Cornell University Press, 1991, pp. 86–98

Hester, D. A., 'Law and Piety in the *Antigone*', *Wiener Studien*, 14, 1980, pp. 5–11

——, 'The Central Character(s) of the *Antigone* and their Relationship to the Chorus', *Ramus*, 15, 1986, pp. 74–81

——, 'Sophocles the Un-philosophical', *Mnemosyne*, xxiv, 1971, pp. 11–59

Kott, J., 'Why Did Antigone Kill Herself?', *New Theatre Quarterly*, 9, 1993, pp. 107–9

Murnaghan, S., '*Antigone* 904–20 and the Institution of Marriage', *American Journal of Philology*, 107, 1986, pp. 192–207

Neuburg, M., 'How Like a Woman: Antigone's Inconsistency', *Classical Quarterly*, 40, 1990, pp. 54–76

Pozzi, D., 'The Metaphor of Sacrifice in Sophocles' *Antigone* 853–856', *Hermes*, 117, 1989, pp. 50–5

Seaford, R., 'The Imprisonment of Women in Greek Tragedy', *Journal of Hellenic Studies*, 110, 1990, pp. 76–90

Segal, C. P., 'Sophocles' Praise of Man and the Conflicts of the *Antigone*', in Woodard, op. cit., pp. 62–85

Shelton, J.-A., 'Human Knowledge and Self-Deception: Creon as the Central Character of Sophocles' *Antigone*', *Ramus*, 13, 1984, pp. 102–23

Sourvinou-Inwood, C., 'Assumptions and the Creation of Meaning: Reading Sophocles' *Antigone*', *Journal of Hellenic Studies*, 109, 1989, pp. 134–48

——, 'The Fourth Stasimon of Sophocles' *Antigone*', *Bulletin of the Intitute of Classical Studies*, 36, 1989, pp. 141–66

Wilkins, J., and Macleod, M., *Sophocles' 'Antigone' and 'Oedipus the King'*, Bristol, Bristol Classical Press, 1987

Modern reception of *Antigone*

Burian, P., 'Tragedy Adapted for Stages and Screens: The Renaissance to the Present' in P. E. Easterling (ed.), *The Cambridge Companion to Greek Tragedy*, Cambridge, CUP, 1997, pp. 228–83

Hegel, G. W. F., *On Tragedy*, ed. and trans. A. and H. Paolucci,

New York, Harper and Row, 1975

Macintosh, F., 'Tragedy in Performance: Nineteenth and Twentieth-century Productions' in P. E. Easterling (ed.), *The Cambridge Companion to Greek Tragedy*, Cambridge, CUP, 1997, pp. 284–323

Mackay, L. A., 'Antigone, Coriolanus and Hegel', *Transactions and Proceedings of the American Philological Association*, xciii, 1962, pp. 166–74

Steiner, G., *Antigones*, Oxford, OUP, 1984

Websites

http://duke.usask.ca/porterj/skenotheke.html: 'Skenotheke: Images of the Ancient Stage' provides valuable visual evidence of stagecraft in classical times

www.apgrd.ox.ac.uk: 'The Archive of Performances of Greek and Roman Drama' contains useful information on the reception of Greek drama in modern performances (reviews of productions, books, current research, events)

http://www2.open.ac.uk/ClassicalStudies/GreekPlays/index.html: also useful on the reception of Greek drama

http:/www.didaskalia.net/index.html: electronic journal on Greek and Roman theatre

http://depthome.brooklyn.cuny.edu/classics/dunkle/tragedy/index.htm: general introduction to Greek tragedy

http://www.theatron.co.uk/: a virtual reality tool for teaching and researching theatre history

Translator's Note

Sophocles English'd

'Bless thee, Bottom, bless thee, thou art translated,' cries the literary-minded Peter Quince, when he sees his noisy amateur actor friend's earnest bonce metamorphosed into a braying ass-head – and Shakespeare's pun is exact: translation – particularly the translation of poetry – involves a fundamental metamorphosis of form. A poem may be written in blank verse, rhyme royal or *terza rima,* but even closer to the heart of the matter is the language it is written in. The words themselves are the underlying form of a poem, because it is only in the actual and precise choice of words that meaning and association, and feeling and music and shape, and all the other elements that go to make up a poem – reside. That is why genuine translation, the lateral movement of something called a poem from one language across to another, is impossible. It can only be transformed, re-shaped in a quite new formal structure, ass-head instead of man-head: and then, if it is any good, it becomes pure ass, essentially asinine, with only the memory of the man remaining. A good poem translated, must become a good poem in its new language, not merely a memory of the old. When Brecht was up before the un-American activities committee, a committee-man solemnly read out a translation of one of Brecht's poems, as evidence of his Communist connections. 'Mr Brecht,' accused the committee-man, 'did you write this poem?' 'No,' replied Brecht, 'I wrote a very similar poem, in German.'

In fact, it is this dilemma that makes the impossible art of translation so endlessly rewarding. If it were simply a matter of transferring blocks of meaning from one language to another, we would programme our computers, and leave them to get on with it. But good translations, because they must live in their new linguistic surroundings, express as much of the translator as of the translated. We read Pope's Homer and Dryden's Virgil for Pope and Dryden, not Homer and Virgil: and who could deny that Tony Harrison's *Oresteia,* controversial as it is in its individuality, is as much a part of Tony Harrison's struggle to bring the northern voice into its own in modern English poetry, as it is a version of Aeschylus?

The truth of the matter is that translations serve as many different purposes as there are translators, and at least four major kinds can be identified. The first is the literal translation, or crib, staff and companion of generations of students, good old indispensable Loeb. These are usually written in an execrable alien English, never spoken or even written anywhere else by the inhabitants of this planet, and full of words like 'suppliant', 'filet' and 'hecatombs', precise enough renderings of Greek and Roman realities, but utterly incomprehensible as lived English.

The second kind is the most ambitious, and the most common: the attempt to render as much of the poem as possible in the new language, trying to reproduce meaning, verse form, style, and even the musical movement of the original. This was attempted on an heroic scale by Dorothy L. Sayers' version of *The Divine Comedy*, but it can easily collapse into a twisted unidiomatic mish-mash, a game for contortionists, tying an elegant human shape into ugly knots in the pursuit of the impossible.

In the third kind of translation, the translator allows himself a considerable amount of freedom, to express the spirit rather than the letter of the original text. His main concern is to recreate the feel and impact of the original as completely as he can, and he allows himself the freedom to travel quite far from the original writer's literal meaning and style: but his overall intention remains to get as close to that original writer as he can, and he still sees himself as servant rather than master. Pope and Dryden might reasonably be described as translators of this kind, and Ezra Pound's aggressively slangy version of *The Women of Trachis* joins that company in kind if not achievement.

The fourth kind, imitation, or re-composition, is effectively the creation of a new work, based on or inspired by an original text in another language, and it is here perhaps that the finest poetry is to be found – many hundreds of Elizabethan love sonnets, Johnson's *London* and *The Vanity of Human Wishes,* imitated from Juvenal, Pope's *Imitation of Horace,* and more recently, Robert Lowell's *Imitations.* We can't go to such poems for anything resembling a version of the original text, more often a perceptive commentary on the nature of the two cultures and ages compared: in Johnson's case, with the insight of genius.

Where does my own translation of the Theban Plays stand? The answer is not quite in any of the four sections, though perhaps nearer to the third than any other. What differentiates it from that third section, creating, in effect, a sub-section of its own, is that I have no Greek, and have worked from one specially commissioned literal translation, and a consideration of the work of many of my distinguished predecessors.

Of course, I did not sit down one bright morning and say to myself, 'I don't read a word of classical Greek, I'll translate Sophocles.' Wearing my other hat as a director, I was discussing with the BBC producer Louis Marks, the possibility of presenting some Greek tragedy on television. My main interest at that time was in setting up a production of Euripides' *The Trojan Women.* It hadn't occurred to me to suggest a trilogy of plays, because as a freelance I knew it was unlikely that I would succeed in getting even one Greek play onto television, let alone three. A few days later, Louis Marks rang me with the totally unexpected suggestion that we should tackle the whole *Theban Trilogy*, and my first reaction was somewhere between awe, delight and disbelief: but I soon grasped the point he had perceived, that there would probably be a greater chance of selling a project on this grand scale to the decision-makers in the BBC than there would be of selling them what in television parlance we would call a one-off Greek play. Louis Marks' instinct proved right. Though we were originally given the go-ahead only for *Antigone* – which had an effect on the translation – Louis' careful political instinct managed eventually, over a period of more than two years, to guide the Sophoclean trireme through the dangerous waters of BBC politics, and bring her safely to port.

We then considered what translation to use, and immediately we were confronted with a huge problem, crucial to the success of the whole project. We were both determined to present these wonderful plays, one of the cornerstones of European culture, in such a way as to reveal at least something of their stature, and why they have been considered the yardstick by which drama is measured for 2,500 years. In television, we were both well aware, the problem is enormously magnified by the fact that the vast majority of our audience would know nothing at all of classical Greek drama, and those who did know something of it would probably be prejudiced by the vulgar notion that it is gloomy, boring and out of date. We were quite determined not to talk down or sell Sophocles short. Our productions would have to be convincing and a pleasure to Greek scholars who have spent a life studying the texts, and a thrillingly compelling new world opening up for viewers to whom Attic tragedy wasn't even a name.

Though television is a good medium for genuine dramatic poetry, it is merciless with any kind of stilted language, and it soon became clear to us that we could present none of the existing translations of the Sophoclean trilogy with the faintest chance of the particular kind of success we hoped for.

At this point, I decided that I ought to do the job myself. The playwright-translator without the original language is a not uncommon figure now, and in poetic drama, where the quality of the language is of the greatest importance, he has even more justification for his existence than in more naturalistic forms. The idea had already been mooted in our earliest discussions about *The Trojan Women*. At that time I had had sixteen of my own original TV plays presented, as well as nine stage plays in theatres around the country, and I had already written and directed the first TV play to be written in verse, *The Testament of John,* though it had not yet been transmitted. Louis Marks had himself been the producer on several of these plays, including *The Testament of John,* and he was very happy to agree with the idea. We discovered, to our amazement, that as far as our researches could probe, the whole *Theban Trilogy* had never been translated complete by a working playwright. It had been left to Greek scholars and poets to do the job. But these great works were written for public performance in a well-established and highly competitive theatre, by men who were themselves poets, singers, actors, composers and dancers, as well as directors of their own plays. That fact convinced me. It was surely time for a playwright to get a look in, even if he did have no Greek.

Before I set a word on paper, I bumped into my friend the actor Patrick Stewart. I mentioned that I was just about to begin translating Sophocles, and I was very surprised when he made a wry face and said he didn't much like Greek tragedy. I was astounded at this in so distinguished an actor, and one, too, so eminently well suited to Greek roles, and I said so. He replied that he had been in many productions, but had always found that the plays were difficult to act well because the actor found himself again and again involved in tremendous dramatic situations which were expressed in the most banal language, and that he himself could never find a satisfactory way of marrying the power of the situations to the poverty of the words. No more useful comment could have been made to me as I began the huge project. I determined that whatever else I did, and however much of a limitation my lack of knowledge of the Sophoclean original was bound to be, I would at least make sure I gave the actors some decent English words to say.

About one thing I was quite clear from the beginning: that these plays are non-naturalistic poetic drama, at the very highest level of the art, certainly the equal of Shakespeare, and that the poverty-stricken speech of modern naturalism, particularly the film-based television variety, would have no place in my versions. That I would write in verse was not a matter of choice, but the point I started from.

When I wrote *The Testament of John*, I had already confronted the problem that faces every twentieth-century English writer attempting drama in verse, namely, what verse form to use. I was quite convinced that the standard iambic pentameter is no longer a possibility in drama. Shakespeare, Milton, Wordsworth and Keats have done all there is to be done with that particular music: for me, at least, their shadow is far too large. So I looked back at the last successful attempt to write verse drama in English, and saw T. S. Eliot. I find his drama very unsympathetic, nor do I see in it any evidence that he possessed those particular qualities which make a writer a playwright. He seems to me to be a part of that long tradition in English letters of major poets who were fascinated by the drama without having any aptitude for it, and the plays he wrote and had successfully performed, a triumph of sheer intellect, a great poet's attempt to do something for which he was fundamentally unsuited. But nevertheless, he had been the first poet-playwright to confront the problem of a suitable verse form for modern drama; he too had rejected the iambic pentameter, and whatever the limitations of his plays as plays, he had created many passages of fine dramatic verse: so I decided to try to use his form to serve my own purposes.

Eliot had created a verse line, loosely based on Anglo-Saxon poetry, but without the alliteration, a line consisting of four feet, in which each foot had to contain one strong beat, but could contain any number of weak ones. In doing so he created a verse movement close to the rhythms of natural speech, with something of the flexibility of prose, but which, with the regular beat of its four stresses, clearly defined a recognisable verse music. The problem this metre sets a writer, one which I have not overcome, is that many lines remain ambiguous in stress, clear enough in the poet's mind perhaps, but capable of more than one kind of scansion. In spite of my strictures, the reader will find plenty of iambic pentameters in the five thousand-odd lines of verse in this book. But the experience of directing these translations suggests to me that the problem is an abstract one, more apparent than real. In the mouths of actors, it tends to disappear. The skill involved, as in all dramatic verse, is for the playwright's instinct for natural stress in dramatic English to coincide naturally and without strain with the formal pattern of the verse: and the freer that pattern, the finer the poet's ear must be. This was the metre I had attempted with *The Testament of John*, so it was natural that I should use it for the dramatic trimeters of Sophoclean tragedy. I decided not to be absolutely strict with myself, and to allow the occasional two- or three-footed line if I wanted it. But I tried to make sure that I only used the shorter line for positive effect, not simply because I couldn't think of any way of filling up the odd feet!

The lyric verse in these plays confronts the translator with his biggest problem, but here my experience as a theatrical practitioner helped me. As a director, I had already decided how I intended to present the choral odes. They had to create a quite new lyrical dramatic experience, utterly differentiated from the dramatic episodes. So Sophocles' formal odes would not be broken up, shared out between the chorus actors and spoken as individual lines, to make them seem as naturalistic as possible. I would use a chorus of twelve (Sophocles himself increased the number of the chorus from twelve to fifteen, but I decided upon twelve because it is divisible by six, four, three, two and one, and would therefore make more interesting formal groupings) and the characters would speak to the accompaniment of live specially composed music, in unison, as individuals, and in all the possible sub-groupings. My lyric verse had to be English lyric verse, with its own life and vitality, so this meant that my models had to be not the Greek originals, whose texture was beyond my comprehension anyway, but the masters of English lyric verse, Keats, Shelley, Marvell, Donne, Jonson, the Cavalier poets, the young Milton. I would try to write tightly rhyming verses, using metres and verse movements imitated from these masters, and I would strive most of all to make these odes convincing as dramatic lyrics in their own right. Where Sophocles in a chorus or choral dialogue repeated the metrical form of a strophe with an exactly similar antistrophe, so I would repeat my lyric verses with meticulous accuracy, strictly reflecting metrical form and rhyme scheme. I would be particularly careful to avoid the use of thunderous full rhymes all the time, using half-rhyme, and even quarter-rhyme – the matching of final consonants only – to ensure flexibility and avoid musical banality. This was not an original decision, I knew. Many translators have tried to rhyme their choruses, using these or similar techniques. But I knew of none that had attempted it with the thoroughgoing concern for form that I intended: nor, indeed, any that were really good enough as English lyric verse. Yeats, of course, made famous versions of choruses from *Antigone* and *Oedipus at Colonus,* but they are a long way from Sophocles, Yeatsian poems in their own right, based on Sophoclean ideas, rather than usable translations.

But that strategic decision left a whole series of tactical questions unanswered. Lyric metres are used in Greek tragedy in a whole series of different ways, in the entry song of the chorus (*parados*) in the choral odes (*Stasima*), the choral dialogues (*kommoi*), in the *exodos,* which often takes the form of a choral dialogue, and even, in moments of excitement, within the dramatic episodes themselves. As a point of principle, I decided that whenever Sophocles used lyric verse, I would use my English lyric form, but I very soon discovered that this decision had considerable implications. Most of the greatest moments – one might almost say all of them – in these three plays are written by Sophocles in the form of choral dialogues, an interaction, in lyric verse, between the chorus and one or two of the main characters. Oedipus' re-entry blinded, his recital of his woes at Colonus, Antigone's farewell to the chorus, Antigone's and Ismene's threnody for the dead Oedipus, and Creon's dirge over his dead son and wife, are all cast by Sophocles in the form of *kommoi*, or formal choral dialogues, often with the most sophisticated poetic skill, in the exact repetition of metrical patterns from verse to verse, and in the breaking up of single lines between several voices. But these sections are usually translated either into prose, or into a loose free verse, with scarcely any differentiation made between them and the normal dramatic episodes. It immediately became clear that these sections represent the moments of the most intense grief and sorrow in the plays, and it is here that the poet has chosen to stylise his work most completely, to remove it utterly from the prosaic world of daily speech – which had little enough part in the world of Greek tragedy anyway – into the world of music, poetry and dance, a world in which grief can be expressed in its purest, most essential form. The wrong kind of naturalism is the greatest danger for twentieth-century actors and directors when attempting the Greeks. That kind of thinking would require Oedipus simply to mutter 'Christ, my eyes hurt' and fall down the steps when he enters blinded. The very fact that he does not say that, but utters a lyric poem, to music, is the essence of the kind of play we are dealing with. Here, too, was the answer to the subversive question that Patrick Stewart had planted in my mind. A tremendous situation requires tremendous things to be said, requires a poem of despair or suffering, upon which the actor can launch himself, and take wing. So the choral dialogues too would have to be written in tightly rhyming lyric verse, and acted to music. The further I looked into this, the more interesting the idea became. It is not only moments of grief and sorrow that Sophocles renders in his *kommoi*, but moments of high drama, like the climax of the row between Oedipus, Creon and Jocasta in *Oedipus the King*, and Creon's seizure of Oedipus in *Oedipus at Colonus*. These, too, most modern translations render in an informal, 'naturalistic' way, and these too I decided to translate into lyric verse, and act to music.

This decision had further implications. I had never intended to attempt to reproduce anything of Sophocles' own verse movement, music or texture – indeed, as a non-Greek reader, it was impossible that I should. But the decision to render such a large part of the plays into lyric verse meant that the translation must necessarily become freer. In the irreconcilable conflict between a literal rendering of all the subtleties of Sophocles' original, and the severe demands of English rhyming lyric verse, the needs of the latter would have to come first, if I was to avoid desperate convolutions and unidiomatic phraseology. My version of the choral odes and dialogues, if it was to do any sort of justice to Sophocles' drama by creating passages of striking, and emotionally moving English, might have to do less than justice to his words. In practice this has meant the occasional use of metaphors not in the original, and the pursuit of ideas or the completion of concepts which Sophocles has not pursued or completed. Simply, there were times when I let my pen have its way, to complete the poem as my instinct told me it had to be completed, and the reader must be left to judge to what degree this is acceptable. Transformation is required, not transliteration. We need a new English poem, full of its own energy and vitality, not a pale reflection of the old.

*

Style was an equally crucial consideration, though here it was easier to see the road that had to be followed. We had decided on a new translation in the first place because we couldn't find one that was written in direct, modern theatrical English, the language employed by the best practitioners on the modern stage. We wanted no archaisms, no inversions, no puffing up of the emotions by Victorian rhodomontade. The great moments had to be earned, through a simple, strong, concrete, metaphorical English, with no vulgar indulgence of modernity or affectation of the ancient. The ambition was to make the language and the ideas expressed within it, as simple, direct and powerful as it must have been to its original spectators, and if this meant a simplification of mythological nomenclature, and the insertion of a few words or lines to make clear an idea that has not survived the journey of 2,500 years, so be it. Two simple examples will suffice. The Greek gods are invoked by many different names, expressing different elements of the same deity, but I have tended to use only one. Apollo remains Apollo, not Phoebus, the Delian, the Archer King, Loxias, or whatever. More importantly, in *Antigone,* all the original spectators would have known the horrific significance of a body remaining unburied – namely, that there was no chance of peace in the underworld until the correct rites had been performed. Creon is damning Polynices' eternal soul, as Hamlet or Isabella might have put it, as well as his body. Sophocles nowhere says this, because all his audience knew it, but I have inserted a line or two in the earlier part of the play to make the tragic issue quite clear.

The actual usage of words is always the most personal matter in any writer's style, and in this way my own verbal personality must be reflected in every line of the play. One of the clearest indications of this is perhaps in the use of certain modern words which in the purest sense would be considered anachronisms. Rumour, in *Colonus*, travels 'faster than an Olympic champion', and Eurydice in *Antigone* remarks that 'We are bred to stoicism in this family'. Zeno of Citium began to develop stoic philosophy a clear four generations after Sophocles' lifetime, and the Olympic Games began in the eighth century BC, many hundreds of years after the Heroic age. But the word 'stoicism' in modern English has nothing at all to do with the philosophy of Zeno. The word has become a part of general modern usage, representing endurance of an intense and uncomplaining kind; just as the phrase 'Olympic champion' doesn't represent to us anything specifically Greek, nor even a specific modern champion, an Ovett or Coe, but the idea of world supremacy in sport: in this particular case, the fastest. People who object to such usages will probably also object to words like 'realpolitik', 'security police', and Antigone's description of Hades as 'that bleak hotel which is never short of a room': but I stand by my usages. In performance they work well, expressing in a vivid modern way an idea that does not seem un-Sophoclean. They are I suppose the standard-bearers or forlorn hope of my attack on the problem of style. My loyalty, as a translator of a text written for performance, must always be principally to the language being translated into, not the language being translated from. That is where my attempt will succeed or fail, not in the details of my treatment, or maltreatment, of the original.

One external factor had an effect on these translations. I was originally commissioned to translate all three plays, and I worked on them in story order, beginning with page one of *Oedipus the King*. Most of the problems of form and style were confronted within the process of translating the first play, but obviously I learned as I went along. I didn't feel that I had really learned how to translate the formal odes and choral dialogues until I was about halfway through *Colonus,* and when I looked back on the completed first draft, it seemed to me that *Antigone* was, by a long way, the best of the three, as by that time I was confident in what I was doing. In these first drafts, I had made no attempt to reproduce exactly the formal patterns of the choruses and choral dialogues. I had allowed my own verse forms to emerge naturally, and simply repeated them where repetition was required. The passages of stichomythia likewise, I kept as sharp as I could, but did not attempt to reproduce the formal one-line or two-line patterns of the original. My translations came out quite a lot longer than the originals, of course, but I had expected that. Part of the greatness of any poet lies in his compression of language, and I knew that that was one of many areas where I couldn't hope to be in Sophocles' league.

It was decided to produce *Antigone* first. In the light of advice from Geoffrey Lewis, my classical mentor, I made several crucial retranslations, but *Antigone* went into production much as originally drafted. A year passed before the next two plays were scheduled for production, and during that time I did a great deal of revision and retranslation. I had always been dissatisfied with the first half of *Oedipus the King*, and while reworking it, I found that I was in fact capable of making versions of Sophocles' odes which were much closer to Sophocles' own length, and I soon discovered the delights of reproducing the stichomythia patterns exactly. When I moved onto *Oedipus at Colonus*, I was very conscious that I was courting disaster by letting the English play become too long. The original Greek text is the longest in the canon, and my first version sprawled to some two-and-a-half hours playing-time. So I took a deep breath and decided to attempt to do all the choruses, choral dialogues, and stichomythic passages in the same numbers and patterns of lines employed in the original Greek, which, although I could not read it, was always at my elbow, so that its formal patterns, or those of them that can be clearly seen on the page, were clear to me. My versions are still longer, of course, even when I employ exactly the same number of lines as the original Greek: but they are not so much longer as to threaten the plays' structure, and the formal patterns, in *Colonus* at least, are absolutely reproduced. In this formal respect, *Colonus* is the closest of the translations. *Oedipus the King* is almost as close, and *Antigone* is the freest of the three. [. . .]

'A poem,' as Auden said, 'is never finished. You simply stop working on it.' The needs of production gave me an unavoidable deadline, but all three plays have been allowed the luxury of some degree of retranslation after the productions. In the first two plays only the odd line or phrase has been changed, but in *Antigone,* the degree of reworking has been considerable.

Sophocles is one of us, not one of a lost them, buried in centuries of dust in forgotten libraries. He is alive now, he lives in our world, and because he is alive, his ideas have changed subtly over the centuries, as mankind has acquired more experience against which to measure his work. Because he was one of the greatest of theatrical artists his work stands up to this scrutiny of the succeeding generations, and as we bring to it our own experience, it becomes richer and more revealing. So there must be nothing archaeological about the act of translation, nothing of the creation of vanished historical epochs. We owe him the best, most idiomatic, up-to-date language we can manage, so that the burning immediacy and power of his art can strike us as powerfully as they struck his contemporaries. My main aim in making this new version of these much-translated works has been to make them seem that they were written not 2,500 years ago, but the day before yesterday, today, and tomorrow.

ANTIGONE

CHARACTERS

ANTIGONE }
ISMENE } the daughters of Oedipus

CREON, King of Thebes

HAEMON, his son

TEIRESIAS, a prophet, blind

A SOLDIER

A MESSENGER

EURYDICE, wife of Creon

CHORUS of Senators of Thebes

GUARDS

SOLDIERS

ATTENDANTS

TEIRESIAS' BOY

This translation was commissioned by BBC Television and first produced in the autumn of 1986, with the following cast:

ANTIGONE	Juliet Stevenson
ISMENE	Gwen Taylor
CREON	John Shrapnel
HAEMON	Mike Gwilym
TEIRESIAS	John Gielgud
SOLDIER	Tony Selby
MESSENGER	Bernard Hill
EURYDICE	Rosalie Crutchley
CHORUS	Patrick Barr, Paul Daneman, Donald Eccles, Robert Eddison, Patrick Godfrey, Ewan Hooper, Peter Jeffrey, Noel Johnson, Robert Lang, John Ringham, Frederick Treves, John Woodnutt
TEIRESIAS' BOY	Paul Russell
GUARDS	Chris Andrews, Steve Ausden, Leon Ferguson, Stephen Epressieux, Steve Ismay, Paul LeFevre, David Rogue, Steve Roxton
ATTENDANTS TO EURYDICE	Jeannie Downs, Vanessa Linstone
ATTENDANTS	Michael Eriera, David Fieldsend, William Franklyn-Pool, Paul Holmes, Jack Lonsdale, Bernard Losh, Graeme Sneddon

Directed by Don Taylor
Produced by Louis Marks
Designed by David Myerscough-Jones
Music by Derek Bourgeois
Costumes by June Hudson

The scene is set outside the royal palace of Thebes. Enter ANTIGONE *and* ISMENE. *They are both nervous and troubled.* ANTIGONE *looks round to be sure they cannot be overheard before speaking.*

ANTIGONE. Ismene listen. The same blood
Flows in both our veins, doesn't it, my sister,
The blood of Oedipus. And suffering,
Which was his destiny, is our punishment too,
The sentence passed on all his children.
Physical pain, contempt, insults,
Every kind of dishonour: we've seen them all,
And endured them all, the two of us.
But there's more to come. Now, today . . .
Have you heard it, this new proclamation,
Which the king has made to the whole city?
Have you heard how those nearest to us
Are to be treated, with the contempt
We reserve for traitors? People we love!

ISMENE. No one has told me anything, Antigone,
I have heard nothing, neither good nor bad
About anyone we love – not since the battle
I mean, and the terrible news
That both our brothers were dead: one day,
One battle, and fratricide twice over,
Each brother cutting down his own flesh . . .
But the army from Argos retreated last night,
I have heard that. Nothing else
To cheer me up, or depress me further.

ANTIGONE. I thought you hadn't. That's why I asked you
To meet me here, where I can tell you everything
Without any risk of being overheard.

ISMENE. What is it then? More terrible news?
Something black and frightening, I can see that.

ANTIGONE. Well, what do you think, Ismene? Perhaps
You can guess. We have two brothers,
Both of them dead. And Creon has decreed
That a decent burial shall be given to one,
But not to the other. Eteocles, apparently,
Has already been buried, with full military honours,
And all the formalities due to the dead

Meticulously observed. So that *his* rest
In the underworld among the heroes is assured.
But Polynices, who died in agony
Just as certainly as his brother did,
Is not to be buried at all. The decree
Makes that quite plain. *He* is to be left
Lying where he fell, with no tears,
And no ceremonies of mourning, to stink
In the open: till the kites and vultures
Catch the scent, and tear him to pieces
And pick him to the bone. Left unburied
There is no rest for him in the underworld,
No more than here. What a great king
Our Creon is, eh sister?
It's against us, you realise, and against me
In particular that he has published this decree.
And he'll soon be here himself, to make it public
To the senators, and anyone who may not have heard it.
He isn't bluffing. He means to act
To make it stick. The punishment
For anyone who disobeys the order
Is public stoning to death. So that's the news,
And you know it now. The time has come
For you too to stand up and be counted
With me: and to show whether you are worthy
Of the honour of being Oedipus' daughter.

ISMENE. Wait a minute Antigone, don't be so headstrong!
If all this is as you say it is,
What can I do, one way or the other?

ANTIGONE. Just say you will help me. Commit yourself.

ISMENE. To do what? Something dangerous?

ANTIGONE. Just to give me a hand to lift the body.
It's too heavy for me to move on my own.

ISMENE. To bury him you mean? In spite of the decree?

ANTIGONE. He is my brother. And like it or not
He's yours too. I won't betray him
Now that he's dead. No one will ever
Throw that in my face.

ISMENE. You must be mad!
Creon has publicly forbidden it.

ANTIGONE. He can't forbid me to love my brother.

He has neither the right nor the power to do that.
ISMENE. Have you forgotten what happened to our father?
Contempt and loathing from everyone,
Even from himself, that was his reward.
And blinded too, by his own hand.
And his mother-wife, as ill matched with him
As those two words are with each other,
She knotted a rope, and hanged herself.
And now our two brothers, both in one day
Caught in the same trap, claiming
Blood for blood and death for death
Each one at the expense of the other.
We are the last ones left, sister,
And what a death is promised for us,
More terrible than any, if we break the law
By defying the king, and the power of the State.
Think for a moment Antigone, please!
We are women, that's all. Physically weaker –
And barred from any political influence.
How can we fight against the institutionalised strength
Of the male sex? They are in power,
And we have to obey them – this time
And maybe in worse situations than this.
May god forgive me, and the spirits of the dead,
I have no choice! State power
Commands, and I must do as I am told.
When you are powerless, wild gestures
And heroic refusals are reserved for madmen!
ANTIGONE. Don't say any more. I won't ask again.
In fact, if you were to offer help now,
I would refuse it. Do as you please.
I intend to bury my brother,
And if I die in the attempt, I shall die
In the knowledge that I have acted justly.
What greater satisfaction than that,
For a loving sister to embrace a loving brother
Even in the grave: and to be condemned
For the criminal act of seeing him at peace!
Our lives are short. We have too little time
To waste it on men, and the laws they make.
The approval of the dead is everlasting,

And I shall bask in it, as I lie among them.
Do as you please. Live, by all means.
The laws *you* will break are not of man's making.

ISMENE. I reverence them. But how can I defy
The unlimited power of the State? What weapons
Of mine are strong enough for that?

ANTIGONE. Fine. That's a good excuse. I'll go
And shovel the earth on my brother's body.

ISMENE. I'm frightened, Antigone. I'm frightened for you.

ANTIGONE. Don't be frightened for me. Fear for yourself.

ISMENE. For god's sake, keep it quiet. Don't tell anyone.
I'll keep our meeting secret.

ANTIGONE. Don't you dare!
You must tell everybody, shout it in the streets.
If you keep it secret, I shall begin to hate you.

ISMENE. There's a fire burning in you Antigone,
But it makes me go cold just to hear you!

ANTIGONE. I'm not doing it to please you. It's for him.

ISMENE. This obsession will destroy you! You're certain to fail!

ANTIGONE. I shall fail when I have failed. Not before.

ISMENE. But you know it's hopeless. Why begin
When you know you can't possibly succeed!

ANTIGONE. Be quiet, before I begin to despise you
For talking so feebly! *He* will despise you
Too, and justly. You can go now. Go!
If I'm mad, you can leave me here with my madness
Which will doubtless destroy me soon enough.
Death is the worst thing that can happen,
And some deaths are more honourable than others.

ISMENE. If you've made your mind up . . . Antigone, it's madness . . .
Remember, I love you . . . whatever happens . . .

Exit ANTIGONE *and* ISMENE *in opposite directions.*

Enter the CHORUS OF THE SENATORS OF THEBES.

CHORUS. The life-giving sun has never shone
More brightly on the seven gates of Thebes
Than he shines this morning:
Never a more glorious dawning
Than this sunrise over Dirce's river,
When the army of the foreign invader
At first light

Made its panic-stricken flight,
And all its white shields and its bright weapons were gone.
Like a snowy eagle from the mountain crest it came
Shrieking down on our city,
The army of Argos, with a spurious treaty
To enforce Polynices' claim,
All its horsehair plumes nodding together
And a grinding of brass and a creaking of leather.

By our seven shuttered gates it waited,
Eyes glittering in dark helmets,
Swords drawn, spears couching.
But before the killing and burning,
The metallic taste of blood
And crashing stonework and blazing wood,
They turned and fled, the music of death
In their ears, at their backs, the dragon's breath.
Zeus had seen them, he who hates inflated
Pride, and the empty boast
Of the windbag, he heard their singing
As if the victory were theirs for the taking,
And he brought down his thunder on their glittering host,
Struck them with lightning, and sent them flying,
Scorched them, and burned them, and left them dying.

Down like a rock from the mountain crest
He came thundering to earth, the flame
Dashed from his hand,
The son of Thebes whose best hope of fame
Was to conquer his native land
And who failed in his quest.
For the war god gave us his word of command,
Like a battle chariot his terrible name
Ran them down where they stood, and they died in the dust.
Now, at each of our seven gates
A Theban defender waits
As seven champions bring their fame and armour to the fight:
And before the coming of night
Six have put their fame to the test,
Six have laid both fame and armour to rest
As a tribute at great Zeus' feet.

At the seventh gate two brothers meet
Sharing their blood in death as in birth,
Each striking together,
Each laying the other
Dead on the earth.

There will be victory celebrations today
In this city of charioteers,
And singing in the streets.
There will be ceremonies of thanksgiving, and grateful tears
For the end of fighting, as the enemy retreats
And the time comes for relaxation and play.
Now, as all voices are raised, and the drum beats
The ecstatic god himself will appear,
Bacchus the drunkard, to take power for one day
In the city he calls his own. Time to dance all night,
To shake the foundations, till the faint light
Of dawn flushes the windows, and the lamps fade.
Now Creon is king. He made
The most of his fortune, and the gods' choice,
The son of Menoeceus. As the people rejoice
The new king enters to take his throne,
The responsibility his alone.
But why has he called us here, to debate
In emergency session
His public proclamation
So vital to the State?

CREON *enters, well-guarded by soldiers.*

CREON. Senators: our country, like a ship at sea,
Has survived the hurricane. The gods, who sent it,
Have navigated us into calmer waters now.
I have chosen to summon this assembly
Because I know I can trust you. Your predecessors
Were loyal and reliable in King Laius' time,
And when King Oedipus, in his exceptional wisdom,
Restored the fortunes of this city.
When tragedy struck him, and his rule was ended,
Your loyalty to the blood royal
Was never questioned, and you supported his sons:
Till they too were brought down,
In a single day, incestuously murdered,

Each brother shedding a brother's blood.
By that same bloodright, as next of kin,
I claim the throne, and all its power
Both city and kingdom. I claim it and hold it
From today, as mine by right.
There is no certain measure of a man's quality,
The depth of his intellect and the maturity of his judgement,
Until he is put to the supreme test
By the exercise of lawful power in the State.
My own opinion is well known:
The ruler who fears the consequences
Of his actions, or who is afraid to act openly,
Or take the good advice of his senators,
Is beneath contempt. Equally contemptible
Is the man who puts the interests of his friends,
Or his relations, before his country.
There is nothing good can be said of him.
Let me make it plain, before the gods,
Whose eyes are in every council chamber,
When I see any threat to this nation,
From whatever direction, I shall make it public.
No one who is an enemy of the State
Shall ever be any friend of mine.
The State, the Fatherland, is everything
To us, the ship we all sail in.
If she sinks, we all drown,
And friendship drowns with us. That's my policy:
A policy of service to the Commonwealth.
And in pursuance of that policy,
I have issued an official State decree
Concerning the sons of Oedipus.
Eteocles, who died fighting for his country,
And with exceptional bravery, we shall bury him
With all the honours and funeral ceremonies
Customary for a man who died a hero.
The other, the outcast, the exile –
His brother Polynices, who returned here
At the head of a foreign army, to destroy
His homeland, to burn down the city
And reduce the people to a condition of slavery,
Or kill them in the streets – I have ordered

That he is to have no grave at all.
No one is to bury him, or mourn for him.
His body is to be left in the open, uncovered,
A stinking feast for the scavengers,
Dogs and crows, a sight to inspire terror.
I intend to make it quite plain
That never, under my administration,
Will people who commit crimes against the State
Reap any benefit from their actions: and at the expense
Of honest decent citizens too.
But people who serve the State, alive
Or dead, that makes no difference –
I shall honour them for their patriotism.

CHORUS. Son of Menoeceus, you are king now.
You have delivered your verdict and sentence
Upon the man who defended the city
And the man who attacked it, unambiguously.
The full power of the law is in your hands,
And it binds the dead, as well as the living.
We are all at your disposal.

CREON. Make sure
Then, that my orders are carried out.

CHORUS. Younger men than us should implement your policies.

CREON. I don't mean that. Polynices' body
Is already under guard.

CREON. What else
Must we do? What other responsibility
Do you lay upon us?

CREON. Not to intrigue
With dissidents, or subversive elements.

CHORUS. We are not mad sir. We know the law,
And the penalty for breaking it.

CREON. Which will be death. And be in no doubt
I shall enforce it. Because there are always men
Who can be bought, who will risk anything,
Even death, if the bribe is large enough

Enter a SOLDIER *in a dusty uniform, struggling with the guards, who bring him before* CREON. *He is very frightened.*

SOLDIER. My Lord Creon . . . sir! If I can hardly speak
For lack of breath . . . it's not 'cos I ran . . .
I kept on stopping, as a matter of fact,

Half a dozen times, and I hung about
As much as I dared. I haven't thought about anything
So much for a long time. 'Listen, don't hurry,'
I said to myself, 'the chances are,
Poor sod, you'll cop it when you get there.'
But then I said to myself, you see,
'Hang about,' I said, 'or rather, don't,
Because if Creon hears this from somebody else,
You're really in trouble.' So I hurried here
As slow as I could, going round and round
In circles, in my head, as well as with my feet!
It's funny how long a mile can take you
When you're thinking what I was thinking. However
Duty called in the end, and I reckoned
It would be safer to face it out.
It may be unimportant, but I've come here,
So now I'll tell you. If I'm punished for it
The gods'll be behind it, that's for sure.
So I wouldn't have escaped it anyway.

CREON. Talk sense, man. Why are you frightened?

SOLDIER. Well, first of all sir, for myself, like,
My own point of view . . . I never done it,
And I didn't see who else done it neither.
So I shouldn't be punished for it, should I?

CREON. Is there any need for all this preamble?
You take great care to dissociate yourself
From what you say: it must be bad news.

SOLDIER. It is bad news sir: and I'm so scared.
I don't know how to put it for the best.

CREON. The plainest way. And then we can have done with you.

SOLDIER. Straight out with it then. The body's buried.
Someone or other. A handful of dust,
That's all, dry dust, but properly sprinkled,
You know, religiously – and then gone –
Whoever it was.

CREON. Do you know what you're saying?
Who has dared to disobey my orders?

SOLDIER. No way of knowing sir, we've no idea!
There had been no digging, no spade marks or nothing.
The ground's rock hard. No wheel tracks either,
From a chariot, or cart, or anything.

In fact, no clues of any kind at all,
Nothing to tell you who might have done it.
When the sentry taking the early turn
Discovered what had happened, and reported back,
We were all shattered, and scared stiff.
It was as though the body had disappeared –
Not buried in a proper grave, I don't mean,
But lightly covered with a layer of earth.
Almost as though some passing stranger
With a religious turn of mind, knowing
That being left unburied means everlasting
Anguish, and wandering without rest,
Had scattered a few handfuls. There was no tracks
Of animals either, not of dogs or anything,
Who might have gnawed at it, and covered it over
With their front legs, like they do a bone.
A real row started then, I can tell you.
We shouted at each other, and it could have been a fight,
There was no one there to stop us. Any one of us
Could have done it, we all suspected each other:
But we all denied it, and there was no evidence
To prove one man guilty rather than another.
So we all dared each other to swear
To go through fire and water, to hold
Red hot pokers in our hands, and call all the gods
As witnesses that we hadn't done it,
And didn't know anyone who had,
Or would even think of it, let alone do it.
And none of any of it got us nowhere.
Then one of the fellers had his say, and he
Scared us all shitless, I can tell you.
He said – and we knew he was dead right –
There was no way out of it, we had to do it
And take our chances – this feller said
'One of us lot must tell the King,
Because we can't just hide it, can we?'
That's what he said. And we knew he was right.
So we decided we'd have to draw lots,
And, just my luck, I drew the short straw.
So here I am. And I don't like telling it
One little bit more than you like hearing it.

The bloke who brings bad news never gets a medal.
CHORUS. My Lord Creon, this policy of yours
Has worried me from the start. My political instinct
Tells me that this may be some sort of warning
Or sign, and perhaps from the gods.
CREON. How dare you!
Shut your mouths, all of you, before I lose my temper!
And you, if you are a superannuated fool,
At least don't talk like one. Is it likely,
Remotely likely, that the gods will think twice
Over that pile of stinking meat?
By god, it's blasphemy even to suggest
That they would care a damn whether he was buried
Or not! Let alone grant him an honourable funeral
As though he were one of their principal supporters:
The man who came to burn down their temples,
Plunder their treasuries, pull down their statues
And bring destruction and contempt for their land and its laws.
Do the gods love criminals these days?
Oh no! They do not! But, gentlemen, there are men
In this city, and I have noted them,
A subversive faction, enemies of the State,
A cell of oppositionists, call them what you will,
Who reject the law, and my leadership!
They meet in secret, and nod and whisper
Their seditious talk, and they are behind this,
Any fool can see that. Their bribery
Has suborned my soldiers, and paid for
This demonstration against my authority!
Money, gentlemen, money! The virus
That infects mankind with every sickness
We have a name for, no greater scourge
Than that! Money it is that pounds
Great cities to piles of rubble, turns people
By the millions into homeless refugees,
Takes homeless citizens and corrupts them
Into doing things they would be ashamed to think of
Before the fee was mentioned, until there's no crime
That can't be bought – and in the end
Brings them into the execution chamber.
Well, whoever they are, these men

Who have sold themselves, they'll find the price
Considerably higher than they thought it was!
CREON *speaks to the* SOLDIER.
You! Come here! Get this into your head!
By Zeus, my god, whose power I revere,
I swear to you, soldier, that either you will find
The man who buried Polynices' body
In defiance of my express command
And bring him here – the actual man
Who sprinkled the earth, no other will do,
Standing here, in front of me – or you, soldier,
Will die for it. And death, I promise you,
Will be the least of your punishments.
You will be made a public example –
And interrogated by the security police,
Kept standing, beaten across the feet,
The whole repertoire of special techniques
At which we excel so much – until
You confess the full range of this conspiracy,
Who paid you, how much, and for what purpose.
The choice is yours: and perhaps that indicates
Where your own best interests lie. Crimes
Against the State and its laws, you'll find,
Are very unprofitable in the end.

SOLDIER. Am I allowed to speak sir?

CREON. No!
Why should you speak! Every word you say
Is painful to me.

SOLDIER. Well, it can't be earache,
Can it sir, not what I said!
It must stick in your gullet. Or further down
Maybe, a sort of pain in the conscience.

CREON. Do you dare to answer me back: and make jokes
About my conscience?

SOLDIER. Me sir? No sir!
I might give you earache, I can see that.
I talk too much, always have done.
But the other pain, the heartburn, as it were,
It's the criminal causing that sir, not me.

CREON. You're not short of a quick answer either.

SOLDIER. Maybe not. But I didn't bury the body.

Not guilty to that sir.
CREON. But maybe guilty
Of selling your eyes for money, eh sentry,
Of looking the other way for cash?
SOLDIER. I think it's a shame sir, that an intelligent man
And as well educated as you are
Should miss the point so completely.
CREON. I'm not interested in your opinions!
If you fail to find this enemy of the State
And bring him here to me, you'll learn
That money, from whatever source,
Will certainly not save *your* life!
Exit CREON.
SOLDIER. Let's hope they find him, whoever he is.
But one thing I'm sure of: they won't find me.
I never thought I'd get out of here
Alive. And when I do get out,
Nothing will bring me back again.
I've had an amazing stroke of luck,
And I won't chance my arm a second time!
Exit the SOLDIER.
CHORUS. Is there anything more wonderful on earth,
Our marvellous planet,
Than the miracle of man!
With what arrogant ease
He rides the dangerous seas,
From the waves' towering summit
To the yawning trough beneath.
The earth mother herself, before time began,
The oldest of the ageless gods,
Learned to endure his driving plough,
Turning the earth and breaking the clods
Till by the sweat of his brow
She yielded up her fruitfulness.

The quick-witted birds are no match for him,
Neither victim nor predator
Among the beasts of the plain
Nor the seas' seething masses.
His cunning surpasses
Their instinct, his skill is the greater,

His snares never fail, and his nets teem.
The wild bull of the savage mountain
And the magnificent stag who passes
Like a king through upland and glen,
The untamed horse with his matted tresses
Uncut on his neck, all submit to man,
And the yoke and the bit – and his power increases.

He has mastered the mysteries of language:
And thought, which moves faster than the wind,
He has tamed, and made rational.
Political wisdom too, all the knowledge
Of people and States, all the practical
Arts of government he has studied and refined,
Built cities to shelter his head
Against rain and danger and cold
And ordered all things in his mind.
There is no problem he cannot resolve
By the exercise of his brains or his breath,
And the only disease he cannot salve
Or cure, is death.

In action he is subtle beyond imagination,
Limitless in his skill, and these gifts
Are both enemies and friends,
As he applies them, with equal determination,
To good or to evil ends.
All men honour, and the State uplifts
That man to the heights of glory, whose powers
Uphold the constitution, and the gods, and their laws.
His city prospers. But if he shifts
His ground, and takes the wrong path,
Despising morality, and blown up with pride,
Indulges himself and his power, at my hearth
May he never warm himself, or sit at my side.

ANTIGONE *is brought in by the guards, the* SOLDIER *is with her, a triumphant smile on his face.*

CHORUS (*severally*). But wait! I can't believe my eyes!
Can this be true?
This is Antigone. I recognise
Her as clearly as I can see you.

Her father's destiny
Was suffering and pain
And on all his progeny
Misfortunes rain.
Child, did you openly disobey
The new king's order
And bury your brother?
Do you have to manhandle her this way?

SOLDIER. We saw it! Actually burying the body,
Caught him in the act, as they say, red-handed.
Only it's not a him, it's a her. Where's the king?

CHORUS. Just returning now: when he's most needed.

Re-enter CREON.

CREON. What's all the noise? By the look of things
I'm here not a moment too soon.

He sees ANTIGONE *and the guards.*

What has happened?

SOLDIER. Lord Creon, I reckon it's always unwise
To swear oaths and make promises,
Even to yourself. Second thoughts,
Nine times out of ten, will have their say
And end up by calling you a liar.
It's no time at all since I promised myself
I wouldn't be seen dead here again:
You were that angry with me the last time,
A right mouthful you gave me, more than enough
Thanks very much. But you can't beat
A real turn-up for the book, can you,
There's nothing more enjoyable than a good win
When you're expecting a towsing. So here I am
Again, as the comic said, and my promises
Not worth the air they was spoken with!
This girl's your criminal. We caught her doing it,
Actually setting the grave to rights.
I brought her here, and there was no panic
This time, I can tell you, no recriminations
Or drawing lots! This job was all mine.
I caught her, and I claim the credit for it.
And now, she's all yours. Take her, and accuse her,
Stone her to death, if you like. By rights,
I'm free to go: and well shot of all of it.

CREON. Where did you arrest her? Tell me the details.
SOLDIER. She was burying him. What else is there to say?
CREON. Are you out of your mind? Do you realise
The implications of what you are saying?
SOLDIER. Sir, she was burying the body, I saw her:
The body you ordered not to be buried.
I can't speak plainer than that.
CREON. Did you
Catch her in the act? Did you see her doing it?
SOLDIER. Well, gentlemen, it was like this.
As soon as I got back, remembering
All those threats, or promises you made me,
We brushed all the earth off the naked body,
Which was all wet and beginning to decay
By now, and we sat up on the ridge,
Well to the windward of the stink.
We all kept a sharp eye on each other,
Ready to nudge anyone who dropped off,
And tear him off a strip too. For hours
We sat there, till about midday.
The sun was smack overhead, blazing down,
And the heat was something terrible, I can tell you.
And then, it was as though a whirlwind blew up,
Definitely a twister it was, but localised, like,
And it raised up a dust storm, which swept across the plain,
Tore all the leaves off the trees, blotted out
The whole sky, and completely blinded us.
It seemed like some terrible manifestation
Of the gods, and you had to shut your eyes
To endure it at all. Then, suddenly it stopped,
And when the air cleared, we opened our eyes,
And saw this girl, standing there,
Beside the grave, and sort of wailing,
As though she were in pain, or maybe, anger:
Just like a bird who comes back to the nest
And finds the eggs smashed, or the fledglings gone.
That's what it sounded like. She was standing there,
Looking at the naked body, and screaming,
And cursing the monsters who had done such a thing –
Us, of course. And then she crouched down,
And picked up a few handfuls of the dry dust

And scattered it on him. She carried an urn,
A small ceremonial bronze thing,
And she poured from it, three times, on the dead body –
Honey and wine and stuff in it, I suppose –
All the proper ritual for a funeral, anyway.
Soon as we saw that, we came charging down
And arrested her on the spot. She wasn't
Frightened or anything. She stood her ground.
So then we formally charged her with the crime,
This, and the one before. She admitted
She'd done them both, and we were relieved
To hear that, I can tell you. But sorry
Too, at the same time. It's very nice
To get out of trouble yourself. Not so nice
When you drop someone else up to the neck in it,
Someone you've got no quarrel with.
But still. Your own life comes first, I reckon.
You have to look after number one.

CREON. And you. You with your head down.
What do you say to this accusation?
Do you admit it? Are you guilty, or not?

ANTIGONE. Yes, I'm guilty. I don't pretend otherwise.

CREON. You, soldier, get out. You're cleared of all charges
Against you, and free to go back to your unit.

The SOLDIER *seems about to speak, thinks better of it, and goes, much relieved.*

Now, tell me, a simple yes or no.
Did you hear of my order forbidding the burial?

ANTIGONE. Of course I heard it. How could I not?

CREON. And yet you dared to disobey the law?

ANTIGONE. Yes, I did. Because it's your law,
Not the law of god. Natural justice,
Which is of all times and places, numinous,
Not material, a quality of Zeus,
Not of kings, recognises no such law.
You are merely a man, mortal,
Like me, and laws that you enact
Cannot overturn ancient moralities
Or common human decency.
They speak the language of eternity,
Are not written down, and never change.

They are for today, yesterday, and all time.
No one understands where they came from,
But everyone recognises their force:
And no man's arrogance or power
Can make me disobey them. I would rather
Suffer the disapproval and punishment
Of men, than dishonour such ancient truths.
I shall die, of course, some time,
Whether you make laws or not. If my death
Comes sooner rather than later, I shall welcome it.
My life has been misery – is misery now.
I shall be more than happy to leave it.
There will be no pain, and no despair
In that. But to leave my mother's son
Out there in the open, unburied,
That would have been unendurable,
I could not have borne it. Whereas this
I shall endure. By your judgement
Of course, I'm a fool. But by mine,
It's the judge, not the accused who's behaving foolishly.

CHORUS. This is her father speaking. Stubborn
Like him, she won't give way, not even
With the whole power of the State against her.

CREON. Well, we shall see. Any man can be broken,
And often the most committed and determined
Break soonest. Even iron, you know,
Left lying in the fire too long
Becomes over tempered, and will snap
As soon as a little pressure is applied.
You can break it in pieces. And the wildest horse
In the end submits to the bit and halter
Just like the rest. People without power,
Ordinary citizens, must necessarily obey
Those in authority over them.
This woman is very proud. That was obvious
In the first place when she broke the law,
And is even clearer now. She glories
In the crime she has committed, and insults me
To my face, as well as ignoring my decree.
If she is allowed to flout the law
In this way, all authority

In the State will collapse. I will not have that!
There will be no exchanging of roles here,
Me playing the woman while she plays the king!
She is my niece, my sister's child.
But I am the law. And that responsibility
Is above kinship. Were she even closer,
The closest, my own daughter, my duty
Would be plain. The law has its weapons,
And they will strike, at her,
And at her sister too – her accomplice,
I've no doubt, in this illegal act –
To the full extent of the punishment proscribed.
The other one, Ismene, bring her here.
I saw her in the corridor, talking to herself
And sobbing emotionally, like a madwoman!
Guilty consciences, you see, can never be hidden
Completely, the human face reveals
Conspiracies before they are enacted
Again and again. But there is nothing
More disgusting than the confessed criminal
Who tries to justify his actions,
As this woman has done here today.

ANTIGONE. What more do you want? Kill me, and have done with it.

CREON. Nothing more than your death. That'll be enough.

ANTIGONE. Then what are you waiting for? Nothing you say
Will be of the slightest interest to me,
And my arguments you will not listen to.
I've done what I said I'd do. I've buried my brother.
I aspire to no greater honour, and if
I am to be famous, let it be for that.
All these, these senators of yours,
They all agree with me in their hearts.
But there is no gag like terror, is there
Gentlemen? And tyrants must have their way,
Both in word and action, that's their privilege!

CREON. You are quite mistaken. None of the Thebans
Anywhere in the city, thinks as you do.

ANTIGONE. They all do! But they keep their mouths shut when you're here!

CREON. Not at all! And you should be ashamed
Setting yourself up against the majority,

Disregarding the will of the people!
ANTIGONE. I love my brother. I honour him dead
As I loved him living. There's no shame in that.
CREON. And the one he murdered? Wasn't he your brother?
ANTIGONE. My mother bore them both, and I loved them both.
CREON. If you honour one, you insult the other.
ANTIGONE. Neither of those dead men would say that.
CREON. Eteocles would. His brother was a traitor.
Does he merit no greater respect than that?
ANTIGONE. But he was not an animal. They both died
Together. And they were both men.
CREON. Yes, and the one died defending his country
While the other traitorously attacked it!
ANTIGONE. The dead have their rights, and we have our duties
Towards them, dictated by common decency!
CREON. And if good and bad are to be honoured equally,
Where are our values? Patriotism! Civic duty!
ANTIGONE. Death is another country. Such things
May not be valued there. May even be crimes.
CREON. An enemy is still an enemy. Dead or alive.
ANTIGONE. No, I was born with love enough
To share: no hate for anyone.
CREON. Very well. Share your love by all means,
Share it with the dead. I wish them well of it.
Women must learn to obey, as well as men.
They can have no special treatment. Law is law
And will remain so while I am alive –
And no woman will get the better of me . . .

ISMENE *is brought in under guard. She has been crying, and looks gaunt and worn.*

CHORUS (*severally*). Look Senators, Ismene, weeping for her sister!
Her face is raw with tears,
Flayed with misery!
Her loveliness is scarred now – this disaster
Darkens her fair skin with premonitions and fears
And flushes her cheeks with anguish, not beauty.

ISMENE *is dragged before* CREON.

CREON. And you! Snake! Slithering silently
About my house, to drink my blood
In secret! Both of you the same!
I looked the other way: and like terrorists

You laid undercover plans to destroy me.
Well, do you too confess your complicity
In this crime? Or protest your innocence?

ISMENE. Yes, I confess. If she will allow me
To say so. I was fully involved,
And if she is guilty, so am I.

ANTIGONE. No! That isn't justice! When I asked
For help, you refused me: and so I told you
I didn't want you, I'd do it alone.

ISMENE. But now that you're in danger, Antigone,
I'm proud to stand beside you in the dock.

ANTIGONE. The dead man knows who buried him. What use
Are people who are all words and no action?

ISMENE. Please, my sister, don't despise me!
Let me share the honour and die with you.

ANTIGONE. You've no right to claim the honour for doing
What you were afraid to do. One death
Will be enough. Why should you die?

ISMENE. Because life without you won't be worth living.

ANTIGONE. Ask Creon to protect you. He is your uncle.

ISMENE. Do I deserve such contempt? Do you enjoy
Making fun of me, sneering at my misery.

ANTIGONE. You're right. It's a reflection of my own pain,
If such bitter pleasures are all I have left.

ISMENE. Let me help you then. It's not too late.

ANTIGONE. Save your own life. Do that for yourself
Without any criticism from me: or envy.

ISMENE. For god's sake, Antigone, will you not allow me
Even to share my death with my sister?

ANTIGONE. No. I won't. You chose to live
When I chose to die: and that's the end of it.

ISMENE. But I wasn't afraid to speak! I warned you
That this would happen. I knew how it would be!

ANTIGONE. And most, the majority, would agree with you.
But some would be of my opinion.

ISMENE. But we're both in the wrong, and both condemned!

ANTIGONE. No, you must live. I have been dead
For a long time, inwardly. I am well suited
To pay honour to the dead, and die for it.

CREON. These women are neurotic, lunatics, both of them!
One of them going off her head before

Our eyes, the other one born unbalanced.
ISMENE. Well, are you surprised! Anyone would crack,
The most tough-minded person, under such treatment.
CREON. You lost your senses when you allowed yourself
To be influenced by her lunacy.
ISMENE. There's no life for me here! Not without my sister!
CREON. Don't speak of her. She's as good as dead.
ISMENE. Will you kill the woman your son plans to marry?
CREON. There are other women: no lack of choice
For a young man. Other fields to plough.
ISMENE. But they're devoted to each other. You can't
Change love as you change your clothes!
CREON. No son of mine can marry a criminal.
ANTIGONE. Oh Haemon, when you hear how your father insults you!
CREON. Let him hear. What does his mistress matter to me.
CHORUS. Lord Creon, you insult your own!
They are formally betrothed. Will you tear
The woman from your own son's arms?
CREON. Death parts all lovers, sooner or later.
CHORUS. If that's how the land lies, the poor child's doomed,
Her death warrant sealed and delivered.
CREON. By you, gentlemen, if you remember,
As well as by me. You heard the order,
Agreed it with me, if only by your silence,
Did you not, before the criminal was known?
We'll have no more shilly-shallying. Take them away,
Lock them up, and keep them under close guard.
It's time they understood they are women,
And their proper place in this society.
There's nothing like the immediate threat
Of death to soften up their rhetoric,
And make them look reality in the face.

ISMENE *and* ANTIGONE *are dragged away by the guards.* CREON *remains on stage during the following chorus.*

CHORUS. They can call themselves lucky, the fortunate few
Who live their lives through
Never drinking from the bitter cup of pain.
But when one unlucky family
Incurs the gods' malignity
From generation to generation

They must swallow the bitter potion
Again, and then again!
Just as rollers crash, and seaspray whips
On an exposed beach, and black clouds lower
And the gale from the north screams through frozen lips,
While the sea casts up from its depths a shower
Of pebbles on the shore, and black sand
From the chasms of ocean darkens the strand.

On every descendant of the ancient line
Of Labdacus, divine
And merciless retribution falls.
In the unremembered past
Some unforgiving Olympian cast
The weight of his vengeance on the whole race,
So that agony, destruction, disgrace,
Destroy son and daughter, and darken their halls
With tragedy. The cold hands of the dead
Reach out for the living, and no one is spared.
Another generation sheds its blood,
New light is snuffed out, the young root bared
For the same bloody axe. The characteristic sin
Of Oedipus, arrogance, brings its bleak harvest in.

For Zeus is all-powerful, no man can match him,
He never sleeps, as man must sleep,
And time, which leaves its mark
On fair complexions and dark,
Can never engrave his face, or dim
The brightness of his palace, where the gods keep
Their ageless court, at the utmost peak
Of sublime Olympus. Zeus is master there,
And well did that wise man speak
Who said that past and future time
He holds in his hand by right,
And that those who climb
In their greatness or wickedness
Beyond the permitted height
He brings to destruction and despair.

But all men hope, and some have ambition,

Far-ranging birds that never tire.
Those wings bear some men steadily onward,
But some others aimlessly swoop and glide
Down to frivolous pastures, landscapes of obsession,
Pathways to disaster, and the merciless fire.
And no man can claim to have understood
Hope or ambition, till the flames burn
Under his feet, and the once solid wood
Of his life is reduced to its last condition,
Ashes, and dust. A wise man said
From out of the depths of his inspiration,
When a man commits crimes, and is proud of the action,
A flaming sword hangs over his head:
No future but the grave, and a funeral urn.

HAEMON *is seen approaching.*

Creon, here comes your youngest son.
Is he desperate with grief
That his future bride
Should be so brutally denied,
And all his hopes of happiness gone?
For the last of your sons, what relief
From his consuming fears
And the bitter penance of tears?
Does he come to beg for mercy
For his beloved Antigone?

CREON. We shall know that from his own lips
Without any need of fortune-tellers.

HAEMON *enters and the two men face each other. Both are aware of the delicacy and magnitude of the situation.*

My dear son. I don't doubt you have heard
The news of our final decision, the condemnation
Of the woman you intended to marry. You come here,
I hope, not in any spirit of anger
Against your father, but understanding
That we are always comrades, and my love for you is unshaken.

HAEMON. I know I am your son, Father,
I understand the depth of your experience
In matters of State, and I try to follow
And benefit from it, whenever I can.
Any marriage would be worthless to me
That did not have your approval, and love.

CREON. Good fellow. Hang on to that! A father's opinion
Should always be influential with his son:
And fathers with young sons, when they pray for them,
Ask especially that they should grow up to be
Loyal, obedient, under pressure the first
To strike at their father's enemies,
Just as they are the first to support his friends.
A father whose sons yield no such profits
From the investment of his parenthood
Breeds grief and sorrow as his offspring,
And becomes himself a figure of fun,
Especially to his enemies. Don't be taken in,
Boy. Don't let any woman ensnare you
By exploiting her sexuality, or any of the attractions
That lure infatuated men into submission.
God help the lovesick fool who marries
A dominating woman. Passion never lasts,
And a cold bedroom breeds cold hearts,
Anger, and bitterness, for there's no hatred
So violent as the hatred of two people
Who were once in love. Get rid of her,
My boy, this girl's an enemy, no good
To you, or your best interests. Spit her out like poison!
Let her find herself a husband that suits her
Among the dead. Don't deceive yourself.
She has been openly apprehended
Performing a criminal act against the State.
She is a confessed traitor, and if I
Were to spare her life, I too would betray
The State, and its law, and everything I stand for.
I will not do it. And she must die.
Let her pray to Zeus till she drops,
Let her assert she stands for family love
And ancient virtues, and all the rest of it.
If I tolerate treachery in my own house,
Under my very nose, how can I crush subversion
Anywhere else in the city, or in the State
At large? A man who rules wisely
Within his own family, is more likely
To make sensible judgements in political matters
In his direction of the State. To pervert the law,

To twist it to serve one's own ends
Or the interests of one's relations –
That cannot be allowed, neither in States,
Nor in families: and will not be allowed
By me, in any circumstances.
Unquestioning obedience to whomsoever the State
Appoints to be its ruler is the law
As far as I'm concerned, and this applies
To small things as well as great ones,
Just or unjust, right or wrong.
The man who is firm in his dealings with his family
Will be equally firm in power, his wisdom
Will be equally remarkable, whether as king,
Or indeed as subject. In times of war
And national danger, he will be the man
You can rely on, the man you would feel safe with
Fighting beside you in the front rank
When the battle becomes critical. Indiscipline,
Anarchy, disobedience, what greater scourge
Than that for humankind? States collapse
From within, cities are blown to rubble,
Efficient armies are disorganised,
And potential victory turned to disaster
And carnage, and all by disobedience,
Anarchy, indiscipline. Whereas the well-drilled regiment
That asks no questions stands firm,
Knows nothing, and needs to know nothing, and wins,
Thus saving the lives of millions of honest people.
Authority is essential in any State,
And will be upheld in this one, by me.
There will be no yielding to female fantasies,
Not by so much as an inch. And if we must be deposed,
Let it be by a man's hand, eh son?
Not by a conspiracy of women!

CHORUS. If an old man is fit to judge, Lord Creon,
You have spoken rationally, sensibly, and with the wisdom
Gathered from long experience.

HAEMON. Father, the most enviable of a man's gifts
Is the ability to reason clearly,
And it's not for me to say you are wrong,
Even if I were clever enough, or experienced enough,

Which I'm not. But it's also true to say
That some men think differently about these things,
And as your son, my most useful function,
It seems to me, is to keep you in touch
With what other people are thinking,
What they say, and do, and approve or disapprove of,
And sometimes what they leave unsaid.
The prospect of your disapproval is a great
Silencer of most men's tongues, and some things
Are never said, for fear of the consequences.
But I can sometimes hear what people whisper
Behind their hands: and everywhere, I hear sympathy
Expressed for this unfortunate girl,
Condemned, as she is, to a horrifying death
That no woman has ever suffered before,
And unjustly, in most people's eyes.
In burying her brother, who was killed
In action, she did something most people consider
Decent and honourable – rather than leaving him
Naked on the battlefield, for the dogs to tear at
And kites and scavengers to pick to the bone.
She should be given a medal for it,
Those same people say, and her name inscribed
On the roll of honour. Such things are whispered
In secret, Father, and they have reached my ears.
Sir, your reputation matters to me
As much as your good health and happiness do,
Indeed, your good name matters more.
What can a loving son be more jealous of
Than his father's reputation, and what could please
A father more than to see his son's concern
That people will think well of him?
Then let me beg you to have second thoughts,
And not be certain that your own opinion
Is the only right one, and that all men share it.
A man who thinks he has the monopoly
Of wisdom, that only what *he* says
And what *he* thinks is of any relevance,
Reveals his own shallowness of mind
With every word he says. The man of judgement
Knows that it is a sign of strength,

Not weakness, to value other opinions,
And to learn from them: and when he is wrong,
To admit it openly and change his mind.
You see it when a river floods, the trees
That bend, survive, those whose trunks
Are inflexible, are snapped off short
By the weight of water. And a sailor in a storm
Who refuses to reef his sail, and run
With the wind, is likely to end up capsized.
I beg you Father, think twice about this.
Don't let your anger influence you. If a man
Of my age may lay some small claim
To common sense, let me say this:
Absolute certainty is fine, if a man
Can be certain that his wisdom is absolute.
But such certainty and such wisdom
Is rare among men: and that being so,
The next best, is to learn to listen,
And to take good advice when it is offered.

CHORUS. There's a lot of sense, my Lord Creon,
In what this young man has said: as indeed,
There was in everything that you said too.
The fact is, you are both in the right,
And there's a good deal to be said for either.

CREON. Is there indeed? Am I expected to listen
And take lessons in political tactics
At my age, from a mere boy?

HAEMON. I'm a man, Father, and my arguments are just.
They stand upon their merits, not my age.

CREON. Oh, they stand upon their merits do they? What merit
Is there, please tell me, in breaking the law?

HAEMON. If she'd done something shameful I wouldn't defend her.

CREON. She has brought the law into contempt! That's shameful!

HAEMON. Listen to the people in the street, Father,
The ordinary Thebans! They say she hasn't!

CREON. I have never based my political principles
On the opinions of people in the street!

HAEMON. Now you're the one who's speaking like a boy!

CREON. I'm speaking like a king. It's my responsibility,
And I will act according to my own convictions!

HAEMON. When the State becomes one man it ceases to be a State!

CREON. The State is the statesman who rules it, it reflects
His judgement, it belongs to him!
HAEMON. Go and rule in the desert then! There's nobody there
To argue with you! What a king you'll be there!
CREON. This boy of mine is on the woman's side!
HAEMON. Yes, if *you* are a woman, I am.
I'm on your side Father, I'm fighting for you.
CREON. You damned impertinent devil! Every word
You say is against me. Your own father!
HAEMON. When I know you are wrong, I have to speak.
CREON. How am I wrong? By maintaining my position
And the authority of the State? Is that wrong?
HAEMON. When position and authority
Ride roughshod over moral feeling . . .
CREON. You're weak, and uxorious, and contemptible,
With no will of your own. You're a woman's mouthpiece!
HAEMON. I'm not ashamed of what I'm saying.
CREON. Every word you have said pleads for her cause.
HAEMON. I plead for you, and for myself,
And for common humanity, respect for the dead!
CREON. You will never marry that woman, she won't
Live long enough to see that day!
HAEMON. If she dies,
She won't die alone. There'll be two deaths, not one.
CREON. Are you threatening me? How dare you threaten . . .
HAEMON. No, that's not a threat. I'm telling you
Your policy was misbegotten from the beginning.
CREON. Misbegotten! Dear god, if anything's misbegotten
Here, it's my son. You'll regret this, I promise you.
HAEMON. If you weren't my father, I'd say you were demented.
CREON. Don't father me! You're a woman's plaything,
A tame lap dog!
HAEMON. Is anyone else
Allowed to speak? Must you have the last word
In everything, must all the rest of us be gagged?
CREON. I must, and I will! And you, I promise you,
Will regret what you have spoken here
Today. I will not be sneered at or contradicted
By anyone. Sons can be punished too.
Bring her out, the bitch, let her die here and now,
In the open, with her bridegroom beside her

As a witness! You can watch the execution!
HAEMON. That's one sight I shall never see!
Nor from this moment, Father, will you
Ever see me again. Those that wish
To stay and watch this disgusting spectacle
In company with a madman, are welcome to it!
Exit HAEMON.
CHORUS. Lord Creon, an uncontrollable fury
Has possessed your son, and swept him off like a whirlwind.
A young man's anger is a terrifying thing!
CREON. Let him go and shout his head off about moral this
And decent that, till he raves himself senseless!
The two women are sentenced. It will take more than bluster
To reprieve them, I promise you.
CHORUS. Both of them sir?
You mean to put both of the sisters to death?
CREON. No. You are right. I can take advice.
The one who covered the body. Not the other.
CHORUS. And for the condemned one: what manner of death?
CREON. Take her to some lonely place, rocky,
And unfrequented by anyone. Find a cave
And wall her up in it. Bury her alive:
But with just enough food so that no guilt
For her death will fall either upon us or the State.
She'll have plenty of time to honour the gods
Of the dead there, since they receive
So many of her prayers. They will release her.
And she will learn that worshipping the dead
Is not the business of the living.
Exit CREON.
CHORUS. When the god of unbridled passion makes war
He always wins.
No force on earth can withstand
His powerful, merciless hand.
When the first flowers appear
In a young girl's cheek
The remorseless magic begins:
And then, from the deepest valley to the highest peak
His traps are set,
And no man's sins
Or virtues can keep him from the net.

The mania is universal. The gods themselves run mad.
Men lose their wits, and no one is spared.

When the madness strikes, no one is safe.
The maturest of men
Will commit follies and crimes
Undreamed of in saner times.
What else could provoke this strife
Between father and son, this family divided
And murderous anger between kin?
There is fire in a woman's eye, incited
By such consuming heat,
A man's mind can burn.
Aphrodite shares power with Zeus, her seat
Is at his right hand, her lightning
Strikes to the heart, and its power is frightening.
The doors open and ANTIGONE *enters, heavily guarded. She is dressed in a plain white gown.*

CHORUS. Yet how can we talk of justice
And the needs of the State
While we stand and watch this
Unendurable sight?
My eyes will have their way and weep,
Seeing Antigone, like a young bride
Going to her bedchamber, to marry the dead
And share their everlasting sleep.

ANTIGONE. In all my wanderings, gentlemen, this place
Has been my home. I was born in this city:
And now I begin my last journey.
I look up at the sun in its familiar sky
And feel its warmth on my face
Only to say goodbye.
In the daytime of my life, in mid-breath,
This security policeman, death,
Arrests me, as he arrests everyone, young and old
At home, or in the street. To the cold
Waters of darkness we come, never
To return across that silent river.
No wedding for me,
No music, no guests in the room:
My wedding gift is eternity
In a stone tomb,

My dowry, for ever not-to-be,
Death my bridegroom.

CHORUS. But your action is famous,
In every street
Mouths whisper 'Antigone'.
You go down to the dead
With the promise of glory ringing in your head
And nothing to devalue your beauty.
No sword has scarred you, plague visited:
Unmarked, untouched, you pass
From the dangerous light
Into the safety of eternal night,
Alive, alone, and free.

ANTIGONE. Do you remember the sad story
Of Tantalus' daughter? She was a stranger
From Phrygia, unmarried, like me, in danger
Like mine. She was sentenced to die on the rock
Of Sipylus, and there was no glory
For her, only the endless shock
Of the elements, and the terrible place
Where she was imprisoned: the mountain's embrace
Like fingers of ivy tying her down,
Enclosing, entombing her, and she all alone
While the snows blinded her, and the freezing rain
Whipped her to rags, and exposed her pain
To the naked sky.
What bitter tears she shed
As she slowly turned to stone, and the grey
Rock petrified her by inches, and she died.
Her story is mine. Today
I shall share her rocky bed.

CHORUS. But she was a goddess
Not born for death
Like the children of men
Whose desperate mortality
Is their only certainty.
Will it soothe your pain
To share her destiny,
Or soften your distress
As alive in the earth

You draw your last breath,
To live on in legend and stone?

ANTIGONE. This is a mockery! By everything
The city of our fathers has ever held sacred,
You landowners, you elder statesmen,
You rulers of Thebes, my dying
Is no joke! Am I a figure of fun
To be treated like a child, insulted and humiliated
As I leave you for ever?
Then, forests and meadows, and our Theban river,
Glittering pathway, ceaselessly flowing
From Dirce's death till now, flat lands
Thundering beneath our chariots, you
Must be my witnesses, my only friends
And mourners, as, victimised by an unjust law, I go
To my last home
In the living tomb,
To wait, while the slow darkness descends,
Cold and starving on my stony bed
Halfway between the living and the dead.

CHORUS. No one has ever dared
To go so far before
As you have dared to go.
Now you have stumbled, and stubbed your toe
And will shortly shed your blood
On the marble staircase of the law.
You carry your father's crimes
Like a millstone on your back:
Small wonder, in such times,
If the bones bend, or break.

ANTIGONE. Nothing more painful than that, the remembrance
Of my father's long agony, and the curse
On my suffering family from the beginning.
So much grief from the unlucky chance
Of the son finding the mother's bed, and worse
Than anything, the benighted offspring
Of that unspeakable marriage: and I,
With the others, share that terrible destiny.
Conceived in incest, no repentance
Can soften the punishment: the years
Pass, the agonies increase

And there is no pity for our tears.
No marriage for me, for certain. I shall close
That book for ever,
As I meet my father
And mother in the shades. The weddings will cease.
Marriage to the woman of Argos finished my brother
And finished me too. One death breeds another.

CHORUS. To pay respect to the dead
Is praiseworthy, an act of love,
And religion must have its due:
But no civilised State can eschew
Authority. Laws must be obeyed,
Whether we approve or disapprove.
If you refuse to sanction
The power of the State
By indulging your obsession
You connive at your own fate.

ANTIGONE. Spare me your sympathy,
Weep no false tears,
I know the path that I must follow,
To the sunless country of eternal sorrow,
The bleak waters of eternity,
The unimaginable years.
No grief where none is felt. I shall go alone
And in silence to my house of stone.
Enter CREON, *with his guards.*
CREON. If death could be prevented by singing arias
About it, or other self-indulgent displays
Of grief, this performance would go on for ever,
I've no doubt. But I've had enough of it.
Take her away, lock her up
In her stone vault, with half a mountain
For a roof, then brick up the door! Let her die
There, if she chooses. Or if she prefers,
Let her stay alive in her grave, why not!
Because the grave's the only fit place for her,
Solitary confinement among the dead!
Whatever she does, there will be no guilt
On me, or on the State. Her death's her own.
But there's no place for her among the living.
ANTIGONE. To my grave then. My honeymoon bed.
My prison. My crypt, under the mountain.

My home for the rest of time. I shall meet
So many of my relations there:
We shall all be guests of the sad-faced queen
Of the shadows, Persephone, in that bleak hotel
That is never short of a room. I am the last,
The unhappiest, I think, and the youngest,
Booking in too soon. But my father will be there
To meet me at the door: my mother will smile,
And hug me close, as she always did:
And my brother. He will be glad to see me,
More than all the rest. At each fresh grave
My hands sprinkled the earth, at each
I poured the purifying water,
And made offerings. And for my beloved Polynices,
Whose broken body I set to rest,
I am rewarded with a shameful death.
There are some, I know, more thoughtful people,
Who respect my action. They must justify me.
Not for a husband, you understand,
Not even for a son would I have done this.
If the law had forbidden it, I would have bowed
My head, and let them rot. Does that
Make sense? I could have married again,
Another husband, and had more children
By him, if the first had died. Do you see?
Do you understand me? But my mother and father
Are dead. There will be no more brothers,
Never again. My love had to speak
At Polynices' grave, or nowhere.
And for that terrible crime, my dearest brother,
Creon sentences me to death,
Drags me here, and will shut me away
In a cavern under the mountain, a living death,
In silence and darkness and solitude.
I shall die unmarried, all those pleasures
Denied me, and motherhood denied
Too, no children to love me, to love:
And now, no friends. What moral law
Have I broken? What eternal truths
Have I denied? Yet now, not even a god
Can help me, and there's no man who will,

I'm sure of that. No help, and no hope.
How can there be, when common decency
Has become a crime? If the gods in heaven
Have changed their minds, and this is the way
They order things now, I shall soon know it:
And I shall have learned my lesson the hard way.
But if some others are mistaken,
Let them be punished as I have been punished,
And suffer the injustice that I suffer!

CHORUS. She hasn't changed, even now. The anger
Inside her still blows like a hurricane.

CREON. The sooner she's got rid of, shut up
Out of harm's way, and forgotten, the better.
Tell those guards to get a move on, or they will regret it!

ANTIGONE. That word is my death.

CREON. And now it is spoken.
Don't comfort yourself with hope. There's none.

ANTIGONE. This is the land of my fathers: Thebes,
Built by a god. You see, senators,
My time has run out, there is no more left.
I am the last of the royal blood,
A daughter of kings. And I die *his* victim,
Unjustly, for upholding justice
And the humanity of humankind.

ANTIGONE *is led away by the guards.* CREON *remains on stage.*

CHORUS. Others have suffered, my child, like you:
Upon Danaë too
The same dreadful sentence was passed.
Far from the light of day
In a tower of brass she was shut away,
And that one single room,
Both prison and tomb
Became her wedding chamber at last.
Like you, she was a child of kings,
Yet in her womb the semen of Zeus
Descending in a golden shower
Made a mockery of the brazen tower.
Fate has its own momentum: when things
Must be, they will be. What use
Is power in the State, or wealth,
Massive armies, an unsinkable fleet?

Gods make their entrances by strength or stealth,
And no tombs or towers can keep them out.

The arrogant King Lycurgus discovered
Wisdom, when he angered
The god Dionysus with his railing.
That proud Edonian king
Was punished with madness, and long
Imprisoned in a rocky cell
To endure the private and particular hell
Of lunacy: till the healing
Silence soothed and re-ordered his brain.
He learned there the terrible power
Of the god he had challenged. Ecstasy
Is beyond man's understanding, a mystery
Deeper than reason, which overcomes pain,
And seeks truth in intoxication and terror.
Only a fool would attempt to stop
The Maenads in full flight,
Or silence their ecstatic singing. The sleep
Of reason is not darkness, but another kind of light.

And where the gloomy rocks divide the seas
In Thrace, by the Bosporos,
The savage god Ares
Laughed to see the sons of Phineus
Blinded with a spindle. Nothing could placate
Their vengeful stepmother's hate.
Her bloody needle darkened their eyes for ever,
Blinding the children, as the gods had blinded the father.
From their mother's wedding day, their destiny
Was settled. Their wasted lives
They wept away in sightless misery.
Yet she was descended from the gods. In the echoing caves
Of the north wind she hallooed, as a child,
And on the open mountainside ran wild
With the horses. Man's fate is determined, will not be denied.
The child Antigone pays for the parents' pride.

Enter the blind man TEIRESIAS, *accompanied by his boy. He looks exactly as he did in* Oedipus the King. *Nothing has changed, either in age or dress or manner.*

TEIRESIAS. Senators of Thebes – and your new king, Creon!
We have travelled together, my boy and I,
Sharing one pair of eyes between the two of us –
Which is the way blind men must make their journeys.
CREON. Teiresias! What news brings an old man so far?
TEIRESIAS. Important news, that can't wait:
And advice, which if you're wise, you'll listen to.
CREON. I've always listened: and acted upon it
More than once!
TEIRESIAS. And like a sensible captain
Who values his pilot, you've avoided the rocks.
CREON. I admit it. We all do. We're in your debt.
TEIRESIAS. Then for god's sake, listen to me now.
You're like a man balanced on a razor,
Likely to fall – or cut himself to pieces.
CREON. Are you serious? Any man would shudder
Hearing such things from your lips
That have foretold so many horrors . . .
Tell me what you mean.
TEIRESIAS. Oh yes, I intend to:
Everything my experience of forecasting the future
And understanding symbols has revealed to me,
I will make plain to you. I was sitting
In my usual seat, a place where I can hear
The singing and the secret language
Of the birds, and understand their meaning,
When I heard, quite unexpectedly,
A terrible new sound, like shrieking, or cries
Of anguish, hysterical twittering and whistling
Like the babble of a barbaric language
Only capable of expressing hatred
Or pain. By that, and the wild beating of wings,
I knew the birds were at war. Such sounds
Could mean nothing else. I could well imagine
Their bloodstained beaks and dripping claws,
And that thought disturbed me deeply. At once
I went to my altar to see what I could learn
From the sacrifice by fire. But nothing would burn.
A filthy liquid ran from the flesh
And dropped on the embers – and sizzled and bubbled
Among the ashes. Then the gall bladder burst,

Spurting stinking acid across the meat,
And all the fat melted, and was rendered down
Till the bone was left bare. I saw all this –
Or my boy saw it. He sees for me
What my eyes cannot, just as I see
Things to which other people are blind.
But in that filth I read nothing. The oracle
Was clogged with fat and decay –
And then . . . it was revealed. I understood
That you, King Creon, have decreed this filth
That chokes our altars. The blood and flesh
That decays and stinks there, is the blood and flesh
Vomited from the gullets of dogs
And carrion crows, the blood of Polynices,
The flesh of that unluckiest of the sons
Of Oedipus, still unburied,
And affronting more than our sense of smell.
The gods themselves are disgusted. They reject
Our prayers and sacrifices. How could they do otherwise?
How can the birds sing of anything
But horrors, blown out with this banquet
Of human blood, clogged and stinking,
Till their very beaks drip with it?
My son, listen to me. Any man
Can make a mistake, or commit a crime.
The man who can recognise what he has done,
See that he was mistaken, or morally wrong,
Admit it, and put it right, that man
Proves that it is never too late to become
Wise, and no one will condemn him.
But if he compounds his stupidity
With stubbornness, and an obstinate refusal
To face the facts, he is nothing but a fool.
Is there anyone more stupid than the stupid man
Who cannot see his own stupidity?
Polynices is dead. Don't revenge yourself
On his remains. You can kill a man once,
And once only. Is there any glory
To be gained by defeating a poor corpse?
This is good advice my son, sincerely offered
By someone who wishes you well . . . Take it . . .

CREON. So that's your news, is it, old man.
I am to be the target, am I,
For everyone to shoot at? Well. I am wise too:
Wise to the ways of fortune-tellers,
And the buying and selling you all go in for.
And I'm to be the latest bargain
I see, I'm to be bought and sold
Like silver from the exchequer at Sardis, or gold
From India, I'm to be part of the trade!
Let me tell you this. There is not enough gold
In the world to buy a grave for that man!
If golden eagles should carry him up
By joints and shreds to Zeus,
And spew him in gobbets on the marble floor
Of Olympus, not even that blasphemy
Would be enough to deflect me from my purpose:
Because I know that no single human act,
However much it may degrade the earth,
And the men who perpetrate or suffer it,
Can stain the purity of the ever-living gods!
But, let me tell you this, Teiresias,
A man can fall: he can fall like a stone,
Especially if he pretends to give good advice,
And wraps it up in a profound cloak
Of religiosity, when all the time
Naked self-interest, and the greed for profit
Are the only motives that matter to him!

TEIRESIAS. Are there any wise men left? Anywhere?

CREON. Goodness, how profound! Do you have any more
Thunderous platitudes to follow that one?

TEIRESIAS. Mature judgement cannot be bought.
No treasure is as valuable. And good advice
Is worth more than a fortune to any man.

CREON. And bad advice is worse than worthless,
A disease which infects the wisest of men!

TEIRESIAS. You describe your own symptoms exactly.

CREON. I refuse to become involved in a slanging match
Or quarrel with the recognised prophet of Thebes!

TEIRESIAS. And yet you insult me to my face. You say
My predictions are both false and dishonest.

CREON. That is because all fortune-tellers
Are money grubbers and charlatans.
TEIRESIAS. Kings too have been known to be acquisitive.
CREON. Do you realise the man you are talking to?
I am the king!
TEIRESIAS. You are the king, yes.
My good advice helped to make you one.
CREON. You've had your successes, I know that,
You've been proved right on more than one occasion.
But honesty's another matter. I've never trusted you.
TEIRESIAS. Don't provoke me to tell you everything.
The dark waters of prophecy are better left undisturbed.
CREON. Disturb them, I don't care! Say anything at all,
But say it honestly, not for cash!
TEIRESIAS. Are you really foolish enough to believe
That money has ever been my motive?
CREON. Because my integrity is not for sale!
TEIRESIAS. Listen Creon. This is the truth!
Before many more days, before the sun has risen
– Well, shall we say a few more times –
You will have made your payment, corpse
For corpse, with a child of your own blood.
You have buried the one still living: the woman
Who moves and breathes, you have given to the grave:
And the dead man you have left, unwashed,
Unwept, and without the common courtesy
Of a decent covering of earth. So that both
Have been wronged, and the gods of the underworld,
To whom the body justly belongs,
Are denied it, and are insulted. Such matters
Are not for you to judge. You usurp
Ancient rights which even the gods
Themselves don't dare to question, powers
Which are not in the prerogative of kings.
Even now, implacable avengers
Are on their way, the Furies, who rise up
From Hell and swoop down from Heaven,
Fix their hooks into those who commit crimes,
And will never let go. The suffering
You inflicted upon others, will be inflicted
Upon you, you will suffer, as they did.

Have I been bribed, do you think? Am I speaking
For money now? Before very long,
Yes, it will be soon, there will be screaming
And bitter tears and hysterical crying
In this house. Men, as well as women.
Other cities too, other States,
Will turn upon you for the crime you have committed.
Dogs and vultures will swarm in their streets
Dropping fragments of the unburied man
At corners, on doorsteps, in the public squares.
They will smell the pollution, and turn to you,
Its author! That's all I have to say.
You made me angry, Creon, with
Your crude accusations. So I made you my target:
And like a good marksman, all my shots
Have hit the bull. You can feel them, can't you,
You can feel the pain, like an arrow, here!
Take me home now, boy. Leave him alone
To entertain some younger ears than mine
With his ridiculous outbursts. Either that
Or let him learn maturer judgement
And how a wise man controls his tongue.

Exit TEIRESIAS *led by the boy. The* CHORUS *is appalled, and* CREON *is visibly shaken.*

CHORUS. My Lord, he's gone, promising nothing
But disasters to come . . .
My hair grew grey in this city:
I was dark-haired here, and now I am white,
And in all that time I have never known
Any of his prophecies to be proved wrong.

CREON. Neither have I, man! . . . I know that much
As well as you . . . My mind's torn apart
Like a tug of war, one way, then the other . . .
How can I give way now? But how
Can I stand here like a fool, and wait
Stubbornly for whatever disaster may be coming?

CHORUS. Lord Creon . . . it's time to take good advice.

CREON. Give it then. Don't be afraid. I'll listen.

CHORUS. Release the woman from her underground prison:
And give honourable burial to the dead man.

CREON. Oh, so that's your advice! Total collapse,

Complete withdrawal! Do you all think that?
CHORUS. We do sir. And do it quickly, for heaven's sake!
The gods never move faster than when punishing men
With the consequences of their own actions.
CREON. How can I do it? It's unendurable
To deny every principle and every action
I have stood fast by. But I dare not stand
Against the iron laws of necessity.
CHORUS. Go on sir, do it now, and do it personally,
Not by proxy – with your own hands.
CREON. Yes . . . I'll go, myself, at once!
Somebody, everybody, bring spades and sledge-hammers
Out onto the mountain. I'm coming with you!
If I've changed my mind, I'll act upon it
With exactly the same determination.
I sentenced her, and I'll set her free,
Tear down the bricks with my own hands
If necessary. Perhaps it is wiser
To let the old laws stand. My fear
Tells me it is. And that's a voice
Every prudent man must listen to.

CREON *rushes off in near panic with his soldiers and attendants.*

CHORUS. Great god with many names,
Child of the thunder,
Whom Zeus conceived on Cadmus' daughter
Here in Thebes: Bacchus, Dionysus,
In Italy revered,
And in Demeter's mysterious Eleusis
Both praised and feared,
This is your native city, where the quiet river
Of Ismenus waters the meadows, where the fever
Of ecstasy possesses your womenfolk, your own
Thebes, where the dragon's teeth were sown.

The whole world worships you,
Wine god, intoxicator:
On the two-pronged mountain where the torches glitter
And the nymphs of Parnassus dance: by the pool
Where Castalia's suicide
Made the fountain magical, and the cool
Waters of prophecy reside.

From the impenetrable slopes of Nysa, where the ivy runs wild
And the vines hang thick in your face, come home, Theban child,
Let the world sing its hymns in vain. In the Theban streets
'Hail,' we shout, 'Bacchus, hail.' And the city waits.

Your mother Semele died here,
Incinerated by the fire of the Universe,
Zeus in his splendour. Now in your city
Another disaster threatens, fear
Locks up our tongues, and, like a plague sore on the face,
The State's disease is made public. We have done wrong.
Now the first necessity
Is for healing. From Parnassus' rocky screes,
Or over the sighing waters of the endless seas
Come to us, healer, and heal. We have suffered too long.

All the stars of the galaxy
Whose hearts are fire, throb to your music,
And the remote voices of measureless night
Speak from the depths of their mystery.
Come, with your crazed followers, your lunatic
Women, the wild Maenads, authentic son
Of Zeus. Bring delight,
And dancing till we drop, bring rest, bring peace,
Bring healing and rebirth, let our anguish cease,
Ecstatic god, whose many names are one.
Enter the MESSENGER.

MESSENGER. Senators, listen! Descendants of Cadmus
Who founded our city, and Amphion, who built it,
Good people of Thebes! No man's life
Ever moves smoothly, according to plan.
Who can make judgements, say this is praiseworthy
In human existence, and this is to be despised
When chance rules everything? One moment a man
Rides high on his fortune, and the same moment
He crashes to the depths. Luck, like the tide,
Is certain to ebb, after the flow,
And no man can tell what will happen tomorrow.
Everyone, surely, envied Creon!
He had saved his country from its enemies,
Taken power as king, and his position

In the State was unchallenged. What's more,
He ruled well, with a firm hand, and his son
Was at his side, to help and succeed him.
All that is over now. What life
Can there be, when the things that make life pleasant
Are all destroyed? A kind of death,
Moving and breathing, but not living.
That's how it is for him. Of course,
He's rich, beyond accounting, he's a king
Still, with all the pomp and circumstance
That rank implies. But what's it worth
When all the joy of life is gone?
A shadow, a mockery, a vulgar pageant.
Who can take pleasure in wealth or power
When all happiness is dead in his heart?

CHORUS. More tragedy for this family? Tell us your news.

MESSENGER. They're both dead. And the living must take the blame.

CHORUS. Who killed them? Who's dead? What happened? Tell us!

MESSENGER. The king's son, Haemon. The royal blood
Shed by a royal hand.

CHORUS. His father
You mean? Or his own?

MESSENGER. His own held the sword.
But his father's actions drove it home.

CHORUS. The prophet warned us: and it all came true.

MESSENGER. That's how things are. It's in your hands now.

CHORUS. The doors are opening, look, here's Eurydice,
Poor woman, Creon's wife. Does she know,
Do you think? Has she come here by chance,
Or because she has heard rumours about her son?

Enter EURYDICE *with her women.*

EURYDICE. Gentlemen . . . good friends. My ears caught something
Of what you were saying, a few words
As I opened the door. I was on my way
To offer prayers to Pallas Athene:
We had just drawn back the bolt, when I heard
A few scraps of your conversation: enough
To make me fear what all mothers fear:
An accident, or some disaster to those we love.
I almost fainted. My ladies-in-waiting

Caught me in their arms. Please, speak it out
Plainly, whatever it is. I can bear it.
We are bred to stoicism in this family.

MESSENGER. Dear Queen, whom we all respect . . . I was there,
I saw it all, and I'll tell you
Exactly what happened. There's no point
In trying to soften the blow now
Only to be proved a liar later.
It's best to tell the truth. I went
With the king, your husband, to the edge of the battlefield,
Where we saw the body of Polynices
Still lying where he fell, and in a terrible state:
The dogs had been at him. So we prayed –
First to Hecate, who haunts crossroads
And tombs, and the scenes of crimes committed
But not atoned for, and then to Pluto,
King of the Dead. We asked them to have pity
On him, and on us, and not to be angry.
Then we washed him, or what was left of him,
With holy water, cut fresh branches
To make a pyre, and burned the remains.
Then we shovelled a mound of his own Theban earth
Over the ashes, and when we had finished
We hurried off as fast as we could
To the prison cell furnished with stones
That served as a bridal suite for the girl
Married to death. But before we arrived,
One of the soldiers, with the unenviable job
Of guarding that god-forsaken place
Came running back to tell the king
That he'd heard a terrible noise, like screaming,
From inside the mountain. And as Creon got nearer
He heard it too – faint, but audible,
A kind of weird sobbing, or moaning,
Low and unearthly, as though grief were speaking
Its own naked language. The king groaned
Aloud, and we all heard him say
'Oh, god, this is what I was afraid of.
Am I a prophet too? This path
Up to the tomb, these last few steps,
Are the most agonising journey I shall ever make.

I can hear my son's voice in there!
You, quickly, guards, anybody,
Get inside, squeeze between the rocks.
Where somebody has already forced an entrance,
Get into the main chamber of the cave
And tell me if it is my son's voice
I recognised, or whether the gods
Are playing some brutal game with me!'
So, we went in and looked, as the half-crazed king
Had told us to. And in the darkest corner
We saw her, strung up by the neck, hanging
From an improvised rope of twisted linen
Strips, torn from her own dress. Haemon
Was right beside her, cuddling her body
As it dangled there, sobbing broken-heartedly
At his wife's death, and the marriage bad luck
And his father's cruelty had made certain
Would never take place. When Creon saw them,
He staggered into the cave, groaning
Like an animal, and sobbed aloud, 'My boy,
My poor boy, what have you done?' And then,
'Have you gone mad, coming here? There's nothing
Here for you but death and annihilation
And despair. Come away from there, my son
Come out, for god's sake, I'm begging you,
Come away!' But the boy just looked at him,
And his eyes were terrifying, with an anger
Like I've never seen before. Without a word
He spat in his father's face, and drew
His sword, and lunged straight for the old man.
But Creon was quick, and skipped out of distance.
And the poor lad, hysterical with grief
And self-disgust, held his sword at arm's length
And plunged it between his own ribs.
And then, still conscious, he lifted the girl
Down into the crook of his arm
And cradled her there, in his own blood.
His breathing got harder and shorter, as his life
Flooded away before our eyes, like a fountain,
Soaking her body – so that her white cheeks
Flushed red again with the bloodstains.

EURYDICE *turns and walks out, without hurry. Her women look round, uncertain, then follow her. Some of the* CHORUS *see the exit, and are disturbed. The* MESSENGER *does not see it, and continues telling his story to the rest of the* CHORUS.

So now they're together, two corpses,
Joined in death. He got his marriage,
Poor lad, but it was solemnised in the grave
Where there are no celebrations.
They look like honeymooners, quietly sleeping
Side by side in one bed: evidence
Of the havoc man can bring upon man
By his own pig-headedness and arrogance.

CHORUS. That's strange . . . What do you make of it? . . . His wife
Has gone without a word: giving no indication
Of her own feelings, one way or the other . . .

MESSENGER. It scares me a bit . . . but I'm quite sure
She has good reason. A public demonstration
Of grief would be unlike her. She'll suffer
Like any other mother, for her son's death,
But in private, with her women. She'd never
Do anything foolish or indiscreet,
I'm sure of that. She's far too sensible.

CHORUS. I don't know. Her silence was unnerving,
Dangerously unlike what one would expect.
That sort of silence is sometimes more threatening
Than screaming and tears.

MESSENGER. I'll go in after her:
Just to make sure that grief doesn't tempt her
To anything silly, or excessive. You're right,
The silence was unnerving. She seemed to feel nothing:
And in my experience, that can be dangerous.

The MESSENGER *goes in after the queen. As he does so, the doors open, and servants enter carrying the dead body of* HAEMON *on a bier, closely followed by the distraught* CREON.

CHORUS. Look there! The king is coming:
But not alone.
A silent witness comes before him,
Dead as stone,
Unspeaking evidence that the crime
Like the grief, is all his own.
He suffers now for his wrongdoing.

CREON. Pain . . .
There was hatred inside me, the urge to destroy
Drove me like a maniac, an insane
Plunge towards death – your death my boy.
See here, the killer and his victim!
See here, the father and his son!
I was responsible. My actions killed him.
There is no blame for him, none.
Blasted in the morning of your life,
My hope, my joy,
My hand powered the knife,
My arrogance determined your fate.
CHORUS. You see the truth now, but you see it too late.

CREON. Suffering
Is the only schoolteacher.
The gods have broken my back,
Whipped me like a beast up this stony track
And destroyed my self-respect.
All pleasure, all rejoicing
They have turned to anguish and weeping.
Man is a naked mortal creature:
Affliction is all he can expect.
Re-enter the MESSENGER.
MESSENGER. My Lord, you have suffered enough. But more
Suffering is marked to your name.
One agony lies here in the open,
Another is waiting, the same
Anguish redoubled, behind the door.
CREON. There can be nothing worse. My heart is broken.
MESSENGER. Your wife is dead, the mother of this slaughtered son.
Her wound is fresh, but the breath of life is gone.

CREON. Hades
Is deep, bottomless the abyss of the dead.
Will you kill me too, or bring me to my knees
To suffer longer: beating my head
Insensible with pain? What can you say,
Messenger of death with the sad face
More than you've said already? My way
Is towards the darkness, my case

Can be no worse than it is. Can you kill me again?
I am dead already. Is there more blood,
More savagery, more hacking of flesh, more pain,
First the son, then the mother? No end to this grief?

CHORUS. There's no hiding it now. See for yourself.

The doors open to reveal EURYDICE *dead.*

CREON. Unending
Unendurable pain.
This is the second time I am forced to see
What no man's eyes should ever see,
Even once. Is this how it ends?
Or will there be more torture, more suffering?
A few moments ago my trembling
Arms embraced a dead son.
Now death has snatched the mother from my hands.

MESSENGER. It was there by the household shrine she collapsed,
Still holding the razor-sharp knife. And as darkness
Drew down its slow blinds, and her eyes closed,
She spoke of Megareus who died in the fulness
Of his youth, her elder boy. By his empty bed
She wept, and for the son whose life ended
Today, and with her last, dying breath,
Cursed you as his murderer, who drove him to this death.

CREON. I'm shaking! I shall go mad with this terror!
There must be a sword, somewhere,
A sharp, two-edged knife
To cut away my life.
Living is misery for me now, for ever.
When I look, I see blood everywhere.

MESSENGER. It's no more than the truth I've told.
Her last word
Was to blame you for both deaths, mother and son.

CREON. How did she die? Did she do it alone?

MESSENGER. She heard them weeping for Haemon, cried aloud,
And skewered herself under the heart with a sword.

CREON. She spoke the truth. All the guilt is mine!
I am the murderer. Make that plain.
Somebody, anybody, take me away:
I disgrace the decent light of day.

I am nothing now. I have become nothing.
Nothing can happen to a man who is nothing.
CHORUS. How can we judge for the best
In times like these?
Prompt action is safest.
What more is there to lose?

CREON. Where are you, my friend? Come you shadowy
Messenger who runs faster than the wind,
Wrap me in darkness, as a friend should!
Why waste another day? What good
Is daylight to me? Why should my misery
Darken the face of another dawn? Pull down the blind.
CHORUS. Tomorrow is a mystery. No man can say
What time will make plain. We live day by day.
The future is in greater hands than ours.
CREON. I am nothing. I want nothing. My last, simplest prayers.
CHORUS. No time for prayers now. Too late to pray.
What must come, will come, tomorrow, or today.

CREON. I am nothing. Take me then. The man
Who killed, without knowing it, his wife and son.
Where shall I go then? Left, or right?
All wrong turnings now. Into the night,
Darkness, hide me. There's blood on my hands. My head
Is split, my back is broken. I should be dead.
Exit CREON.
CHORUS. The key to human happiness
Is to nurture wisdom in your heart,
For man to attend to man's business
And let the gods play their part:
Above all, to stand in awe
Of the eternal, unalterable law.
The proud man may pretend
In his arrogance to despise
Everything but himself. In the end
The gods will bring him to grief.
Today it has happened here. With our own eyes
We have seen an old man, through suffering, become wise.
Exit the CHORUS.

Notes

page

5 The first production of this translation was set inside the royal palace as though in a council chamber or senate house. Translation and production were conceived together so Antigone's second speech reads '. . .That's why I asked you/To meet me *here*' rather than the literal '*outside the palace*'. [Translator]

The blood of Oedipus . . . the two of us: according to the myth (see p. xvi), Oedipus killed his father and married his mother. The notion that children must suffer for the crimes of their parents (hereditary crime and punishment) was common in ancient myth and is present in most Greek tragedies (in the *Oresteia* for example, three generations of the same family are tainted and cursed by the gods for having committed a number of horrifying acts). The curse that has shaken the household of Oedipus could suggest that the actions and behaviour of the characters are predetermined and therefore inevitable. However, through the overall portrayal of the tragic figures and their line of thinking through the play, it is difficult to approach them purely as puppets operated by destiny. The concepts of fate and human choice in Sophocles' play are best understood as complementary rather than opposing factors that determine human action.

army from Argos: Argos was a powerful Peloponnesian city-state in Greece and a close ally of Athens. According to the myth, Polynices married the daughter of the king of Argos, Adrastus, who soon after prepared an Argive army to restore his son-in-law to his father's kingdom of Thebes. Polynices and Adrastus were to lead the expedition against Thebes (see p. xvi).

black and frightening: the imagery of darkness (associated with death and bad news) throws into contrast the images of light and sunrise which are used in the choral song soon to follow.

buried with full military honours: in fifth-century Athens and with the development of the democratic city-state, private demonstrations of grief gave way in favour of great public funerals to honour those who died fighting for their city. During the collective burial the bodies of the warriors were carried to the grave, tribe by tribe, on wagons. The whole population was allowed to attend the burial and an orator chosen by the city addressed the people. The most famous example of a funeral speech is Pericles' oration, presented in the work of the historian Thucydides (II.35–46), demonstrating the public projection of the ideals of Athenian democracy.

6 *He is to be left . . . in the underworld*: as in modern times, in ancient Greece burial rites were essential for the dead to find peace. In the proper ceremony, women had a central role. Their responsibilities included intense and physical expressions of mourning (beating breasts, tearing clothes) and the pouring of libations (milk, honey, animal blood) over the tomb. It was believed that if the dead person did not receive a proper burial his restless spirit could come and haunt the living.

public stoning to death: a cruel form of punishment associated with treachery in pre-democratic ancient Greece. The notion of publicly exposing the cause of the city's dishonour and pollution and killing him or her by public stoning was a custom which existed in older days as a rite of purification for the city. (The ceremony took place on the first day of the festival of the *Thargelia*.) In democratic Athens however, political traitors and enemies of the state were normally expelled from the city and sent into exile, losing their citizen status. The decision was made following a democratic procedure.

7 *Caught in the same trap . . . death for death*: in many Greek tragedies the issue of revenge through violent actions results in an inevitable cycle of violence from which the tragic characters cannot escape. Ismene suggests that the only way of breaking this cycle is by listening to Creon and accepting his decree.

We are women . . . madmen!: through this statement Ismene sums up the position of women in Athenian society. Obeying the decree the sisters would be accepting their inferior role as women in a male-dominated society. It seems here that the authority of men is positioned above the authority of the gods who would decree a proper burial. For Ismene heroic refusals are reserved for 'madmen', implying that heroism is not admirable but rather an unbalanced state of mind. On many occasions Antigone is characterised as being 'mad' or 'passionate' by Ismene, Creon and the chorus.

8 *The laws you will break are not of man's making*: this is the first time that Antigone suggests a distinction between natural (divine) and artificial (man-made) law. Natural laws were also described as 'unwritten laws' or 'ancestral laws'. They protected the relationship between kin, hosts and guests, and the living and the dead. Throughout the play Antigone passionately defends the laws of the gods against those made by men.

There's a fire . . . to hear you!: imagery of the senses is characteristic of Sophocles' poetic use of language to raise emotions and feelings in the spectator. Antigone's passion is associated with fire while Ismene's fear makes her shiver.

some deaths are more honourable: heroes and true warriors were very interested in their reputation after life. Achilles (one of the best examples of a true hero) went to war even though he knew he would die, in order to live in the memory of future generations. An honourable death (the last act of one's life) secured an honourable reputation.

Choral song (Victory song): the language contains images of light associated with victory and hope.

Dirce's river: the west river of Thebes. The river is named after the wife of one of the city's early rulers, Zethus. Rivers are very important in local myth and religion (producing fertile land) and are usually associated with a city.

9 *white shields*: Argive soldiers were thought to have carried white shields in battle probably because of a confusion between the city's name Argos and the adjective *argos* which meant 'white'.

Like a snowy eagle: the image of an eagle that attacks the city is associated with military action. The adjective 'snowy' suggests that the eagle was white (see note above). The eagle (Argive army) is described as attacking the Theban dragon. Sophocles uses the traditional enemies of eagle and snake/dragon to illustrate a conflict in the same way as Homer does in the *Iliad* and Aeschylus in the *Oresteia*. The eagle has traditionally been associated with the sky and the dragon/snake with Mother Earth. The Thebans believed they were descended from dragon's teeth which were sown on the ground by the city's founder, Cadmus, and sprang up as warriors.

horsehair plumes: the soldiers' helmets were adorned with horsehair plumes.

seven gates of Thebes: the walls of the actual city of Thebes had seven gates.

Zeus: king of the gods of ancient Greece. He came to power by ousting the previous dynasty of Titans. Zeus is associated with the sky and male authority. His weapon is the thunderbolt.

war god: Ares who was the god of war and martial violence. There was an important cult of Ares in the city of Thebes.

seven champions: Aeschylus earlier treated this story in *Seven Against Thebes* (467 BC), which focuses on the attack on Thebes and ends with Antigone's decision to give her brothers an equal burial. (It is suggested that this final section has been added later, influenced by Sophocles' *Antigone*).

10 *Bacchus*: also known as Dionysus, son of Zeus by Semele. He was the god of wine and theatre. In contrast to Apollo, he is connected with darkness, nature and ecstatic behaviour through collective dancing.

Menoeceus: the father of Creon and Jocasta and a descendant of the Sparti, the armed men who rose from the teeth of the dragon of Ares which had been sown by Cadmus. When the army from Argos laid siege to Thebes, Teiresias foretold that if one of the Sparti sacrificed himself to the god Ares, Thebes would be saved. Menoeceus therefore threw himself from the walls and the Thebans were indeed victorious.

The new king enters to take his throne: it is the usual practice of tragedy to announce the entrance of a new character on stage.

ship at sea: a common metaphor used to describe the city-state in Greek tragedies.

Laius: king of Thebes, son of Labdacus, father of Oedipus, grandfather of Antigone and Ismene (see p. xvi).

11 *as next of kin*: Creon claims the throne due to kinship but, ironically, then disregards the laws of kinship. However, Creon is only related to the sons of Oedipus by marriage, as the brother of their mother. In ancient Greece blood-kinship came only from the father's side.

Is the man who puts . . . before his country: friend (*philos*) in ancient Greek means both 'loved one' and 'close relations'. The conflict between friend and country, individual and state was a strong issue in fifth-century Athens. This is evident in Pericles' funeral speech. Pericles argues that when the whole state is healthy and prosperous the individual profits but when the individual is flourishing the state is not out of danger.

14 *Not buried in a proper grave . . . earth*: though Antigone cannot offer a proper burial ceremony to her brother she knows that even a few handfuls of earth will accomplish the ritual. The sprinkling of dust and pouring of a libation would be enough to allow her brother's soul to rest in peace, as there was nothing more Antigone could do under the circumstances.
Red hot pokers . . . gods: reference to some form of trial through ordeal to prove the truth. Whoever was burnt by the fire or pokers would be a liar.

15 *Money*: the issue of bribing and profit highlights Creon's concentration on the material as opposed to the spiritual world.

17 Choral song (Praise of man): one of the finest lyric examples written on the inventiveness and creativeness of man. The theme of human progress reappears in many dramatic texts of the time, for instance, Aeschylus' *Prometheus Bound* and Euripides' *Suppliant Women*. It has been suggested that all these passages are inspired and based on a work by the philosopher Protagoras entitled *On the Original State of Things*.

21 *A small ceremonial . . . anyway*: a fine description of a traditional burial rite.
Natural justice: see note to p. 8 on law.

23 *But I am the law*: Creon's arrogance is gradually becoming stronger.
tyrants: tyranny in Greece initially meant 'one-man rule' and the epithet 'tyrant' had no negative meaning attached to it. Later on, the word became associated with authoritarianism and oppressiveness (probably due to particular individuals who misused their position as single ruler).

24 *The dead have their rights*: in ancient Greece, the dead were treated as the living. The only difference between the dead and the living was that the former lived in the underworld and could not be seen. However, just like the living, they have rights and duties.
Patriotism! Civic duty!: the main values in the democratic city of Athens, as expressed in Pericles' funeral speech (p. xx).

25 *all words and no action*: the difference between a hero and an

ordinary human being is that the first puts his words into action.

27 *Labdacus*: Oedipus' grandfather, and father of Laius.
merciless retribution falls: for cursed and polluted families see note to p. 5.
Olympian: Mount Olympus, Greece's highest mountain, was the residence of the Greek gods also known as the Olympian gods.

29 *woman . . . exploiting her sexuality*: women's bodies often signal danger for the male spectator. An example of this is Herodotus' famous story of Gyges in which Gyges' act of looking and his sexual desire for a naked woman results in his death.
ancient virtues: virtues of the Aristocratic age (Homer's time).

34 *Exit Creon*: most scholars assume Creon remains on stage throughout the Chorus's and Antigone's threnody. My production proved that Creon's next lines can be played quite as effectively as an entrance as they can as an interruption. [Translator]
god of unbridled passion: Eros who was the Greek god of love and son of Aphrodite. The Greek word *eros* is connected more to sexual attraction than love, an irresistible force which causes madness in its victims. The chorus here sing a song to Eros, reminding the audience that Creon is in danger of offending not only the gods of the underworld but Eros and Aphrodite as well.

35 *Aphrodite*: goddess of beauty and sexual attraction
that silent river: Acheron, a river of the underworld.

36 *Tantalus' daughter*: Princess Niobe. Her father (Tantalus) was the king of Phrygia in Asia Minor and a notable criminal in myth. Niobe was married to an early ruler of Thebes named Amphion. She is believed to have boasted of the beauty of her children, comparing them to Apollo and Artemis, children of the goddess Leto. This infuriated Apollo and Artemis who killed Niobe's children. According to the legend, after the murder Zeus felt sorry for Niobe and turned her into a rock. Sophocles must have intended his audience to think of the last part of the story, the transformation of Niobe.
Sipylus: a mountain in Asia Minor.
goddess: Niobe was a granddaughter of gods.

38 *Marriage to the woman of Argos*: Polynices had married Argia,

the daughter of the king of Argos.

39 *Persephone*: a Greek goddess, daughter of Demeter (the goddess of agriculture) and Zeus. She was the wife of Hades (god of the underworld) and therefore queen of the underworld.

I shall die unmarried: marriage to a Greek woman signalled her passage from being a girl to becoming a woman. Here Antigone emphasises the fact that she will die very young and without having fulfilled her role as a woman.

40 *Thebes, Built by a god*: the city was founded by Cadmus whose wife Harmonia was the daughter of Aphrodite and Ares. Also, the god Dionysus was the son of Zeus and Semele, who was the daughter of Cadmus.

Upon Danaë too: Danaë was an Argive princess, whose father King Acrisius imprisoned her in a tower of brass for fear that her future son would kill him. Aeschylus tells this story in *Suppliant Women* (*c.* 463).

semen of Zeus: Zeus in the form of a golden shower entered Danaë's prison and impregnated her.

41 *King Lycurgus*: king of Thrace (a northern region of Greece), who rejected the worship of Dionysus. As a punishment for this, he was driven to madness, committed various crimes, and ended up imprisoned in a cave. Edonia is in western Thrace.

Maenads: wild women, devotees of Dionysus associated with the worship of the god.

In Thrace by the Bosporos . . . pride: this section refers to the story of Cleopatra, daughter of an Athenian princess, Oreithyia, and the north wind, Boreas. She was married to the King of Thrace, Phineus, with whom she had two sons. It is said that Phineus' second wife blinded Cleopatra's sons and imprisoned her. Another version of the myth recounts that the sons were also imprisoned in a tomb like Antigone.

god Ares: god of war (see note to p. 9).

Teiresias: the blind seer (see note to p. 10). Teiresias also appears in Sophocles' *Oedipus the King*, when he tells Oedipus that it was Oedipus himself who killed Laius. Oedipus refuses to believe him and accuses Teiresias of conspiring against him.

42 *understanding symbols*: the prophets received signs usually from the natural environment and animal sacrifices which they interpreted to foretell the future.

43 *oracle*: the oracle, or mouthpiece of the gods, was consulted at

certain sacred places such as the temple at Delphi. Their incomprehensible words were interpreted by the priests and priestesses there for ordinary morals.

44 *at Sardis*: in Asia Minor. In the river near Sardis, silver was found. Asia Minor was famous for its metals.

45 *the Furies*: divinities whose role was to avenge crimes committed within the family. They were the agents of the 'old law'. In Aeschylus' trilogy the *Oresteia* they appear live on stage and play a key part in the development of the trilogy.

49 *Against the iron laws of necessity*: here Creon gives another name to what Antigone calls the 'natural laws'. These laws are unbreakable. Necessity was the divinity of absolute destiny and like Zeus was a daughter of Cronus.

Great god with many names: Greek gods had various names usually associated with the places they were worshipped and the capacity they had as gods.

Cadmus' daughter: Semele, who was the mother of Dionysus and daughter of Cadmus and Harmonia.

Demeter's mysterious Eleusis: Demeter, goddess of agriculture and mother of Persephone (see note to p. 39). At her shrine at Eleusis (a town close to Athens) there was a famous mystery cult in which Dionysus played a prominent role.

Ismenus: a Theban river after which Ismene is named.

nymphs of Parnassus: it is said that Dionysus held revels on Mount Parnassus. Parnassus is the mountain on which the Delphic oracle was built.

Castalia: a fountain on Mount Parnassus. It was sacred to the Muses. According to legend, Apollo transformed the goddess Castalia into a fountain, whose waters had the power to inspire those who drank them with the genius of poetry. The water was also used to clean the temples at Delphi.

48 *slopes of Nysa*: Nysa is a mountain traditionally associated with Dionysus. Its actual location seems uncertain since it appears in different places in different contexts. Here the reference is probably to a mountain located at Euboea (in mainland Greece), overlooking Thebes.

Incinerated by the fire of the Universe: Zeus' jealous wife Hera persuaded Semele to ask Zeus, who was her lover, to reveal himself in all his glory, knowing that this would cause Semele's death. Zeus did as Semele requested and as a result she was consumed by fire.

Amphion: an early ruler of Thebes.

49 *Pallas Athene*: unwedded goddess born from Zeus' forehead, deity of wisdom and patroness of handicrafts. Though female, she was portrayed dressed in armour and was often associated with martial virtue.

50 *Hecate*: a wandering goddess of the underworld, connected with burial grounds and darkness. Offerings to Hecate were left at crossroads.

Pluto: another name for Hades, the god of the underworld.

52 *A silent witness*: it is perfectly feasible, though not always practicable, for Creon to enter carrying his dead son – in which case this line should be rendered: 'He carries a silent witness with him.' [Translator]

54 *Megareus*: the elder son of Creon.

Questions for Further Study

1. How far do you think that the Greek spectators' familiarity with the story affected their perception of the play?
2. In what ways are Athenian culture, religion and politics reflected in Sophocles' version of the Antigone story?
3. Consider how the ritual and festival context (dances, prayers, sacrifices) of the ancient theatrical performance could have affected (a) the staging of *Antigone*; (b) the audience's perception of *Antigone*.
4. Do you think that the formal ancient theatrical conventions (space, masks, poetic language, chorus, etc.) could still work on an emotional level for a modern audience of *Antigone*?
5. Consider how rhetoric ('the art of persuasion' in public speaking) could have informed or influenced the acting of *Antigone*.
6. How could rhetoric co-exist with masked acting (loss of identity under the mask/persona of the mythical character)? Using *Antigone* as an example in its political and ritual aspects, consider the paradox of acting in ancient Greek theatre (getting lost in the mask/being conscious of performing).
7. Can the spectator identify with the characters in *Antigone*? If so, to what degree and in what ways?
8. The chorus of Greek tragedy has been alternatively described as a 'commentator' on the action and as an 'initiator' of action assuming a more active role in the development of the play. How would you describe the chorus in *Antigone* and how would you stage it in order to highlight its function?
9. Why do you think Sophocles chose to have Antigone killed half-way through the play?
10. Is there a true hero in this play? To what degree does the characters' final destiny affect their heroic status?
11. How important is the issue of divine law in the tragedy? To what extent could a modern spectator appreciate Antigone's decision to sacrifice her life in order to honour the gods and her family?
12. Even though the gods are not physically present on stage they

can still affect the dramatic action. Consider this statement in relation to the play.

13. Consider possible ways of highlighting the political dimension of *Antigone* on stage for a modern audience.
14. How does Creon's relationship to the chorus and the rest of the characters affect our perception of his role as political leader?
15. Consider conflict as a theatrical way of presenting political and ideological views to a democratic audience. Could the exchange of speeches in *Antigone* be compared to a modern political debate?
16. How do the representations of gender in the characters of Creon, Antigone, and Ismene construct and influence the characters' attitudes towards each other?
17. What does *Antigone* tell us about women and their position in Greek society? How does Antigone compare with Sophocles' Electra?
18. In what way could the opposing principles expressed in the play be staged in order to communicate the concerns and contradictions of modern society?
19. What are the major patterns of imagery in this play and how are they connected with Antigone and Creon? How could these be visually highlighted on stage?
20. Does the play present us with a clear view of what is morally right or wrong?

DON TAYLOR was a playwright and poet, and a director of plays in all the media, as well as a translator of Greek drama. In the early 1980s he translated Sophocles' Theban plays: *Oedipus the King*, *Oedipus at Colonus* and *Antigone*. He directed the trilogy for BBC TV and it was broadcast on consecutive nights in 1986. He went on to translate three of Euripides' war plays: *Iphigenia at Aulis*, *The Women of Troy* and *Helen*, the first of which was televised in 1989. His own stage plays include *The Rose of Evam*, *The Exorcism*, *Brotherhood*, *Daughters of Venice*, *Retreat from Moscow*, *When the Barbarians Came* and *The Road to the Sea*. Including works for radio and television, he wrote more than fifty plays and films, among them three verse plays. He died in 2003.

ANGIE VARAKIS received her first degree in Theatre Studies from the University of Patras in Greece and her MA and PhD in Drama and Theatre from Royal Holloway, University of London. Her research interests involve the performance practice of Greek theatre with a special emphasis on the use of masks in modern productions of Greek drama. She has participated in a series of international conferences on the modern staging of ancient drama and contributed to the electronic journal *Didaskalia* and to the forthcoming *Blackwell's Companion to Classical Receptions*, ed. Lorna Hardwick and Chris Stray, and *Arisophanes in Performance, 421 BC–2005 AD: Peace, Birds, Frogs*, ed. Edith Hall, published by Legenda. She is currently lecturing at Royal Holloway, University of London, and the University of Kent at Canterbury.